SLAYING YOUR
GIANTS

SLAYING YOUR GIANTS

BIBLICAL SOLUTIONS TO EVERYDAY PROBLEMS

KENT CROCKETT

HENDRICKSON
PUBLISHERS

Slaying Your Giants: Biblical Solutions to Everyday Problems

Hendrickson Publishers Marketing, LLC
P. O. Box 3473
Peabody, Massachusetts 01961-3473

© 2013 by Kent Crockett

ISBN 978-1-61970-063-5

Revised and updated from the previous title *The 911 Handbook*.

Unless otherwise indicated, Scripture quotations in this book are taken from the NEW AMERICAN STANDARD BIBLE®, Copyright © 1960, 1962, 1963, 1968, 1971, 1972, 1973, 1975, 1977, 1995 by The Lockman Foundation. Used by permission.

Scripture quotations marked NLT are taken from the Holy Bible, New Living Translation, copyright © 1996, 2004, 2007 by Tyndale House Foundation. Used by permission of Tyndale House Publishers, Inc., Carol Stream, Illinois 60188. All rights reserved.

Scripture quotations marked NIV are taken from The Holy Bible, New International Version®, NIV® Copyright © 1973, 1978, 1984, 2011 by Biblica, Inc.™ Used by permission. All rights reserved worldwide.

Scripture quotations marked TLB are taken from The Living Bible copyright © 1971. Used by permission of Tyndale House Publishers, Inc., Carol Stream, Illinois 60188. All rights reserved.

Scripture quotations marked HCSB are taken from the Holman Christian Standard Bible®, Copyright © 1999, 2000, 2002, 2003, 2009 by Holman Bible Publishers. Used by permission. Holman Christian Standard Bible®, Holman CSB®, and HCSB® are federally registered trademarks of Holman Bible Publishers.

Scripture quotations marked KJV are taken from the *King James Version* of the Bible.

Italics in Scripture have been added by the author for emphasis.

Printed in the United States of America

Second printing — October 2013

Cover Art: David and Goliath, illustration from 'Bible Stories', 1968 (colour litho), D'Achille, Gino (20th century) / Private Collection / The Bridgeman Art Library

Library of Contress Cataloging-in-Publication Data

Crockett, Kent, 1952–
    [911 handbook]
    Slaying your giants : Biblical solutions to everyday problems / Kent Crockett.
      pages cm
    Rev. ed. of: The 911 handbook : Biblical solutions to everyday problems. c1997.
    Includes bibliographical references.
    ISBN 978-1-61970-063-5 (alk. paper)
    1. Christian life—Biblical teaching. I. Title.
    BS680.C47C76 2013
    248.4—dc23

                             2012050262

DEDICATION

To my precious wife, Cindy.
You've been my wife, best friend, mother of
our children, counselor to the needy, and
the one who has loved me at all times.
You are Wonder Woman.

CONTENTS

INTRODUCTION   1

CHAPTER 1   HOPELESSNESS   3
             One in a Billion

CHAPTER 2   FEAR   13
             How's Your Nervous System?

CHAPTER 3   DISCONTENTMENT   25
             May I Change Seats, Please?

CHAPTER 4   DOUBT   37
             Without a Doubt

CHAPTER 5   TEMPTATION   47
             Adam and Eve's Instruction Manual

CHAPTER 6   UNFORGIVENESS   59
             Who Is in Your Dungeon?

CHAPTER 7   GUILT   71
               Canceling Guilt Trips

CHAPTER 8   CHANGE   83
               Breaking Out of Comfort Zones

CHAPTER 9   WORRY   93
               The Movies in Your Mind

CHAPTER 10   SELF-IMAGE   103
               I Love Me, I Love Me Not

CHAPTER 11   PESSIMISM   115
               Treasure Hunting

CHAPTER 12   ANGER   127
               Anger Mismanagement

CHAPTER 13   REJECTION   141
               The Angel Inside the Marble

CHAPTER 14   IMPATIENCE   151
               God's Waiting Room

CHAPTER 15   BURDENS   161
               Check Your Baggage Here

CHAPTER 16   DEPRESSION   175
               Singing in the Dark

CHAPTER 17   ENVY   189
               The Possession Obsession

CONTENTS

CHAPTER 18   **JEALOUSY**   199
              A Sneaking Suspicion

CHAPTER 19   **DISCOURAGEMENT**   207
              The End of Your Rope

CHAPTER 20   **DEATH**   215
              Scared to Death

DISCUSSION GUIDE FOR GROUP STUDIES   223

NOTES   241

ACKNOWLEDGMENTS

I would like to express my gratitude to the following:

My Lord Jesus Christ, who saved me and taught me how to solve giant problems.

To Mike and Laurie Mozingo, John and Donnie Mitchell, Randy and Jane Abele, Mike and Donna Murphy, and all the members of Journey Church in Prattville, Alabama, who have supported me.

To Dan Penwell, now in heaven, who took a chance on me and published my first manuscript.

To my friends Paul Baskin and Sterling Myers, and my brothers Stuart and Bruce, for always being an encouragement to me.

To my editors Michelle Rapkin and Barbara Greenman, and the entire team at Hendrickson Publishers.

INTRODUCTION

After Moses split the Red Sea, the children of Israel spent the next forty years wandering in the wilderness. Their ultimate destination was Canaan, so Moses sent twelve men to spy out the land and give a report about what they saw. Ten spies came back with this report:

"All the people we saw were huge. We even saw giants there, the descendants of Anak. Next to them we felt like grasshoppers" (Numbers 13:32–33 NLT).

This was frightening news to those who had dreamed of a problem-free Promised Land. Up until now, they probably assumed they could stake their property claims without any opposition. But after hearing about giants in the land, they now realized that moving into Canaan wouldn't be so easy.

Suddenly it dawned on them: they would have to kill the giants before they would inherit what God had promised. The book of Joshua describes some of the battles they fought as they took possession of the land.

Although many years have passed since this took place, we receive God's blessings in the same way today. First conquer the giants. Then inherit the land.

God could have made it easy for them by driving out all enemies before they got there. But if they didn't fight any battles, they wouldn't need to trust God. Without the struggles of war, their faith would have been weak, and they would not have appreciated what they received.

Today, the Promised Land represents the life that God wants for you in His kingdom—joy, peace, and fulfillment. The "giants" you must defeat are spiritual struggles, negative thoughts, and destructive attitudes, all which try to keep you from enjoying life. Although these aren't physical battles, they are just as real as the ones Israel fought to enter their land.

This book describes some of the prominent giants you will face in life—problems that look bigger and more powerful than you. However, with God's power in your heart and the sword of the Spirit in hand, every giant will fall before you. It's critical that you defeat these invisible enemies; if you don't, you will continue living in misery and turmoil.

I'll teach you how to defeat each problem, but reading how to do it won't be enough. Only you can slay the giant that's attacking you. You can and will win every battle, as long as you are depending on the Lord. He has given you authority over all the power of the enemy, so there's no reason to be afraid.

The rest of your life can be the best of your life. You're writing your own autobiography. You might not have had a good start in life, but you can make a great ending. I hope and pray you'll finish your life well.

Chapter 1

HOPELESSNESS

One in a Billion

And when they came to Capernaum, those who collected the two-drachma tax came to Peter, and said, "Does your teacher not pay the two-drachma tax?" He said, "Yes." And when he came into the house, Jesus spoke to him first, saying, "What do you think, Simon? From whom do the kings of the earth collect customs or poll-tax, from their sons or from strangers?" When Peter said, "From strangers," Jesus said to him, "Then the sons are exempt. However, so that we do not offend them, go to the sea and throw in a hook, and take the first fish that comes up; and when you open its mouth, you will find a shekel. Take that and give it to them for you and Me." (Matthew 17:24–27)

I went to McDonald's the other day. Their latest promotion was the Monopoly game where I had a chance to win $1 million if I could get the winning piece, Boardwalk. When I read the fine print on the official rules, I learned my chance of winning was one in 518,071,190. I figured there was only one winning piece printed for the entire country. Not good odds.

Even though I am not a gambler, I pulled the sticker off my french fries' container to see if I was about to become a millionaire.

Nope. Not even an "instant winner" of a small drink. I got Atlantic Avenue for the fifth time. Wasn't God's will, I guessed.

Maybe your odds don't look too good. You're getting desperate and losing hope. The candle is about to burn out. You are thirty-five years old and still not married. In your mind, the odds of finding Boardwalk are better than finding the right mate.

Perhaps you're climbing a financial mountain of debt that appears to be insurmountable. It could be you're in a situation that seems so hopeless that the solution will require nothing short of a miracle. If God doesn't intervene soon, it will be disastrous. Your predicament appears to be so impossible, it's hard for you to imagine how the Lord could possibly meet your need.

I hope that you'll grasp this important truth about God: He doesn't have to consider the odds when it comes to providing for you. With God involved, the chances of something happening really don't matter. This passage gives us an amazing example of how He can do miracles and provide no matter how impossible the situation may look.

Facts about God

Four facts about God are established in this passage that will help you during your desperate situation.

Fact 1: *God knows your needs before you ask Him.*

Peter received an unexpected bill. One day he was standing outside of the house when the tax collectors arrived. They wanted to know if Jesus was going to pay the tax to support the temple, which was a commandment found in Exodus 30:13. When Peter went into the house to inform Him, Jesus spoke about the tax before Peter could say anything. Even though Jesus wasn't outside to hear the conversation, He wanted Peter to know He had supernatural knowledge of this need even before he asked.

Sometimes we think that the purpose of prayer is to inform God of our needs. We think that He's unaware of what is going on in our lives, and if we don't tell Him, He will never know. We think He's too busy counting hairs on people's heads to be concerned about real needs.

However, Jesus said the Father knows what we need even before we ask (Matthew 6:8). The purpose of prayer is not to inform God about all the things happening in our lives. We pray because God says our prayers will make a difference in bringing things to pass on earth. Some things will not happen unless we pray.

Shortly after Dallas Theological Seminary was founded in 1924, it almost had to shut down. The creditors were going to foreclose at noon on a certain day, and the leaders of the school were desperate. President Lewis Chafer met with his faculty in the office, praying fervently that God would provide. One of the men, Dr. Harry Ironside, prayed, "Lord, we know that You own the cattle on a thousand hills. Please sell some of them and send us the money."

In the meantime, a Texas businessman stepped into the seminary's business office and said, "I just sold two carloads of cattle in Fort Worth, and I feel compelled to give the money to the seminary. I don't care if you need it or not, but here's the check."

The surprised secretary took the check and knocked on the door of the prayer meeting. Dr. Chafer took it out of her hand and discovered it was for the exact amount of the debt. He turned to Dr. Ironside and said, "Harry, God sold the cattle!"[1]

What are the odds of that happening? Without God, one in a billion. But with God, the odds change to one in one. The Lord knew the needs of Dallas Seminary before the faculty asked, and God prearranged for the businessman to sell his cattle and bring in the money.

God is also fully aware of your needs and prepares ahead of time the solution to your problems. And you probably aren't going to figure out how He will do it.

Isaiah 55:8–9 says,

"For My thoughts are not your thoughts,
Nor are your ways My ways," declares the LORD.
"For as the heavens are higher than the earth,
So are My ways higher than your ways,
And My thoughts than your thoughts."

God's IQ is much higher than you could ever imagine.

My little dog Bandit has an IQ of one, maybe two. On a good day he can play dead. Sometimes he will tilt his head and look at me as if he were trying to figure out what I am thinking. But he will never be able to understand my thoughts, because people thoughts are so much higher than dog thoughts.

If I read Bandit every book in my office library trying to educate him, it would be a waste of time. If I opened the hood of my car and tried to explain to him how to repair it, he would comprehend nothing. He isn't capable of understanding these things, because dogs are not as intelligent as people. It would be useless to try to explain things to him that are beyond his ability to grasp.

In the same way that human thoughts are higher than dog thoughts, God's thoughts are higher than our thoughts. We can't comprehend how God supernaturally moves people and events when the situation looks impossible.

How does God cause a businessman to sell his cattle for the exact amount needed at Dallas Seminary, then lead him (without his knowledge of the school's problem) to donate the money right before the bank was about to foreclose? How does He guide two people, who don't know each other and don't know they are being led, to meet at a certain place and eventually get married?

We aren't capable of understanding how God does these things any more than Bandit understands how to read a book or repair a car. But just because we don't understand how God will miraculously come through doesn't mean He doesn't know how He will do it. He is able to do far beyond all that we are able to ask or even think (Ephesians 3:20).

Fact 2: *God controls events that you can't control.*

After Jesus revealed to Peter that He already knew his need, He told him to go to the sea and throw in a hook. When he caught the first fish, he would find a coin inside its mouth that would be used to pay the tax.

Now out of all the ways He could have chosen to meet this need, why did He choose this way? Aren't there easier ways to get money? Of course there are. He did it for a reason. God did it to demonstrate to Peter (and to us) that He controls events that we can't control.

Peter was probably thinking, *Wait a minute, Jesus. I know how to fish better than You do. Remember, I had a fishing business, and the best way to catch fish is to use a net, not a hook.* And Peter was right. It's much easier to use a net to catch fish.

But Jesus told him to use a hook for a reason. He didn't want Peter to catch a whole net full of fish. He only wanted him to catch one fish, the right fish. Out of all the fish in the sea, only one had a coin in its mouth.

If you are single, how are you going to find the right person to marry? There are nearly seven billion people in the world. But remember, you don't need to marry seven billion people. All you need is one. The right one.

The Lord is the only one who knows where that person is. If God can lead a fish to a man, then He can lead a woman to a man—or a man to a woman. Thousands of fish swam in the Sea of Galilee, but Peter didn't need to catch them all. He only needed to catch the one with the coin inside its mouth.

Peter had no control over the fish that he would catch. All he could do was hold the fishing pole and trust what Jesus had said. And God made sure that the right fish would bite on Peter's hook. Imagine being that fish under water trying to locate that tiny hook out of the entire sea. What are the odds of the right fish finding that little hook?

Without God, one in a billion. With God, one in one.

Jimmy Smith, a student at Houston Baptist University, was interested in becoming a missionary. Two missionaries had invited him to visit their work in Guatemala. Money was tight, so he and his wife knew the trip would be impossible unless God intervened.

Several weeks later Smith went fishing with a deacon in his church named Gene Alexander. They talked about an upcoming fishing tournament with a twenty-thousand-dollar prize for catching a particular fish. The deacon knew of Smith's desire to visit Guatemala and said, "I'll give you $5,000 for the trip if I catch the winning fish." Upon learning of the prize fish, Mrs. Smith logged it in her prayer journal and prayed for God to provide.

On the day of the tournament, Gene Alexander cast out his line and reeled in his first catch of the day. When he took the fish off the hook, he was surprised to discover it was marked as the twenty-thousand-dollar-prize fish! Not only did Jimmy Smith and his wife make the trip to Guatemala, they later returned to the country to serve as foreign missionaries.[2]

Officials speculated the odds of landing that fish on his first cast were one in 6.8 billion. But that's without figuring God into the equation. With Him, the odds are one in one.

Fact 3: *God's timing is always perfect.*

Just as we can't apprehend God's thoughts or understand how His sovereignty works, we often miscalculate His timing. Because we are so impatient, we usually think God is either late or has forgotten about us. But God's timing is always perfect.

Peter went to the sea and threw out the line. It was no accident that the right fish was at the right place at the right time. God had set up a divine appointment for the fish to meet Peter when he arrived at the correct spot on the sea.

God specializes in making divine appointments. It was no accident that:

- When Saul was looking for lost donkeys, he met Samuel at the appointed time set by God (1 Samuel 9:3, 15–17, 24).

- The arrow shot by a soldier at random had the correct direction and timing to strike wicked King Ahab in a tiny joint in his armor, which fulfilled a prophecy (2 Chronicles 18:16, 33).

- Mary and Joseph had traveled to Bethlehem for the census at the same time Mary gave birth to Jesus, fulfilling the prophecy of Micah 5:2 (Luke 2:1–6).

- At the exact moment when Peter denied Jesus for the third time, the rooster in the courtyard crowed twice, fulfilling the prophecy of Jesus (Matthew 26:74–75).

- The whale was at the appointed spot in the ocean at the right time to catch Jonah when the men threw him overboard (Jonah 1:15–17).

- The ram was caught in the thicket at the exact moment when Abraham was about to offer up Isaac (Genesis 22:10–13).

- When the disciples entered into the city, they met a man carrying a pitcher of water, who led them to the room for the Last Supper, exactly as Jesus had prophesied (Mark 14:13–16).

This proves that not only is God in control, but He also has perfect timing. He knows the precise moment when He needs to come through.

In the early 1980s, David Smith was the pastor of a small church near Farmington, New Mexico. He faithfully served and sacrificed but struggled financially to provide for his wife and small child on his $600-per-month salary.

One morning his wife, Jackie, pulled the last can out of the cupboard and served him a dish of hominy. He had no money left to buy groceries. Although David had often preached on God's faithfulness to provide, the Lord seemed to have forgotten about them.

David stared at his grits and then gritted his teeth. He could have chosen another profession where he could have made a much larger salary. This wasn't in the agreement when he surrendered to full-time ministry. He got up from the table, bolted through the kitchen door, and stomped across the yard next door to his church office. He was furious and wanted the Lord to know exactly how he felt.

"God, You promised to provide for me, but today we're out of food and money. Where is Your faithfulness that I've been preaching about? Why haven't You come through?"

For the next forty-five minutes, he continued his rant. As he thought about resigning and looking for another job, the phone rang. It was Jackie.

"David, you need to come home right now."

"Why? Is something wrong?"

"You'll see when you get here."

David hurried out of the church, but what he saw stopped him in his tracks. A woman was carrying groceries from her car to his front door. Her station wagon was completely filled up to the roof with cans of food and meat. The only space that wasn't filled was the driver's seat.

"I thought you might need these," the woman explained. "It was on my heart to bring them to you."[3]

The Lord's provision came at the last minute, like the ram caught in the thicket for Abraham. God always does His greatest miracles when things look hopeless. Sometimes He waits until time and resources are exhausted before He provides.

A newly licensed pilot, Franklin Graham, the son of evangelist Billy Graham, was flying from Vero Beach, Florida, to Longview, Texas. He met with bad weather over Mobile, Alabama, and air traffic controllers told him to fly north toward Jackson, Mississippi, to avoid the approaching storm.

As he rose above the clouds, the instrument panel lights flickered. A minute later the radio and instruments went dead; then all the lights went out. Franklin realized he was in a desperate situation, so he asked God to intervene.

He dropped below the clouds, hoping to see the ground. When he spotted the distant lights of Jackson, he headed for the airport's rotating beacon. He circled the control tower and, since he didn't have any electrical power, manually lowered the landing gear.

At that moment the runway's emergency landing lights came on, and he landed. As soon as he was on the ground, the lights went off. *That's odd,* he thought, *at least they could have waited until I taxied to the ramp.*

After he got out of the plane, a man from the tower asked, "Who gave you permission to land?" No one in the tower had seen the small plane circling overhead.

Why would the lights be turned on if they hadn't seen him? They "just happened" to be turned on by an air traffic controller who was explaining to his visiting pastor what he would do in case a plane ever attempted to land without radio communications![4] At the exact moment when Franklin needed the lights, the controller turned them on without knowing the plane was there. What are the odds of that happening?

Without God, one in a billion. With God, one in one.

Fact 4: *God will supply your needs when you obey Him.*

Jesus told Peter to throw the hook into the sea. That's not too difficult. But if he had not obeyed, he would never have caught that fish. It is essential that we fulfill our part in what God asks us to do.

Peter was responsible for only two things. The first thing was to find the right sea. He could have gone to the Dead Sea, but there aren't any fish living in it. It was pretty obvious that wasn't the sea Jesus wanted him to fish in. Some people aren't catching anything because they are fishing out of God's will in the Dead Sea.

The other thing he had to do was throw in a hook. God didn't make the fish jump into the boat. Peter had to throw out a line. Many times when God wants to provide, He asks us to do something, such as throwing out lines.

Peter could have thrown out a net, trying to increase his chances of catching the fish with the coin in its mouth. But if he had done so, he would have been disobedient. Jesus specifically instructed him to throw out a hook. We must obey God, even if it makes better sense to do it in a different way than what He says.

So Peter did it. He threw out his line into the sea and waited for a nibble. After a few seconds, he noticed his cork begin to bob and then disappear under water. He pulled back on his pole, lifting the fish out of the sea and into the boat.

When he opened the fish's mouth, he discovered a coin inside. It was the exact amount needed to pay the tax for both Jesus and Peter. The only way it could have been more miraculous would have been if he had taken the coin out of the fish's mouth, and the fish had said, "Ta-da!" The right fish was at the right place at the right time with the right amount. God's divine appointments never disappoint.

But there's one more question we need to answer. How did the coin get in the fish's mouth? Did God create the money in its mouth?

I don't think so. If Jesus was going to create money, He could have turned a couple of flat stones into coins and handed them to Peter. Besides, it would have made Jesus a counterfeiter if He had created the coins, because it wouldn't have been the official currency of the government.

No, someone in a boat on the Sea of Galilee either threw a coin into the water or accidentally dropped a coin overboard. As it drifted toward the bottom, the fish caught it in its mouth and, without swallowing it, kept it there until Peter threw in his hook and caught him. What are the odds of that happening?

Without God, one in ten billion. With God, one in one!

Chapter 2

FEAR

How's Your Nervous System?

"Do not tremble or be dismayed, for the LORD your God is with you wherever you go." (Joshua 1:9)

When Max Wilkins was a boy, he visited his great aunt Ruth overnight. He was always a little bit afraid to sleep there because she lived in an old three-story house, where the floors creaked like a haunted house in the movies.

That night he went to his bedroom on the third floor and climbed into bed. The room was dark, but enough light was coming through the window that he could see a man standing in the corner of the bedroom!

Max was absolutely terrified. He knew that if he tried to make a run for the door, the man could easily catch him. He figured the only thing to do was to lie still and pretend to be asleep. All night long he lay in bed with one eye open, ready to run if the man made a move.

He kept still for hours until the sun came up. As it got brighter in the room, he could see that the man in the corner . . . was just a coatrack with a hat on it.[1] He spent a night in torment because he believed something that wasn't true.

Although some fears are based on reality, most are just coat racks with hats on them. Fear and worry are usually nothing more than our imaginations out of control.

One of the scariest giants you'll ever face is the giant of fear. That's his job—to scare you away from the Promised Land. Joshua discovered this after he took over the leadership of Israel after Moses died.

It's his first day on the job, and he has to lead a nation into battle to fight the Canaanites, Amorites, and Hittites. Put yourself in his shoes. This wasn't a video game where no one gets hurt. We're talking hand-to-hand combat with real swords. Real spears. Real arrows. Real blood.

God gave Joshua a pep talk to calm his nerves:

> "Just as I have been with Moses, I will be with you; I will not fail you or forsake you. Be strong and courageous, for you shall give this people possession of the land which I swore to their fathers to give them. . . . Have I not commanded you? Be strong and courageous! Do not tremble or be dismayed, for the LORD your God is with you wherever you go." (Joshua 1:5–6, 9)

God told Joshua, "When you face your new assignment, be aggressive and bold. When you meet the enemy face to face, don't let your knees knock or your hands shake. You don't need to be afraid because I will be with you."

The same God who spoke those words to Joshua several thousand years ago wants to speak them to you today. And the message is the same. Before you can fulfill what He wants you to do, you must conquer your fears.

Laughing at Fear

Some people deal with their fears by making fun of them. One of the fads back in the 1990s was No Fear shirts, which had different sayings written on the back, challenging the people reading them to not be afraid. Here are some of the quotes from those shirts:

It must be hard living without a spine. No Fear

FEAR

It takes a big man to cry, and even a bigger man to make him cry. No Fear

There's no such thing as unnecessary roughness. No Fear

Bull riding. Where your only friend is a guy dressed up like a clown. No Fear

For every battle there is a price to pay. Now pick up your teeth and go home. No Fear

Fear tastes like chicken. No Fear

It's not whether you win or lose. It is whether I win. No Fear

First Prize. All the marbles. Second Prize. A set of steak knives. No Fear

The Road to Victory is paved with flesh and bones. No Fear

It's a dog eat dog world and the scared are wearing Milkbone underwear. No Fear

You do not greet death, you punch him in the throat repeatedly as he drags you away. No Fear

And finally, the one I like best. It just says, "Thou Shall Not Fear."

If God were to give out No Fear shirts back then, that's the one He would have given to Joshua. That's the one that He wants you to wear: Thou Shall Not Fear.

Thou Shall Not Fear moving to a new city, because I'm leading you.

Thou Shall Not Fear losing your job, for I am your employer.

Thou Shall Not Fear hard times, for I will take care of you.

Thou Shall Not Fear the future, because I am waiting for you there.

Thou Shall Not Fear death, because I am eternal Life.

Fear Is an Assumption

What is the meaning of the word *fear*? Dean Martin once said, "Show me a man who doesn't know the meaning of the word fear, and I'll show you a dummy who gets beat up a lot."

Fear is actually negative faith. It's faith in reverse gear. Faith and fear have something in common. They both make assumptions about what will happen. Faith assumes that good things are going to happen, while fear assumes the very worst will occur. You get to choose which assumption you'll believe.

If fear were logical, we could talk ourselves out of it every time. When facing death or tragedy, we could simply say to ourselves, *This threat isn't real, so I'm not going to be afraid.* If logic or reasoning could conquer the giant of fear, no one would ever be frightened. Of course trying to talk ourselves out of being afraid never works. Conquering fear requires a more powerful weapon than logic.

There's no rhyme or reason to fear because it affects everyone differently. What one person is afraid of, another person isn't. Some people are tormented when they must fly on an airplane, while others take flying lessons as a hobby. In an interview aboard Air Force One, President Ronald Reagan was asked if he had overcome the fear of flying.

"Overcome it?" he retorted. "I'm holding this plane up by sheer will power."[2]

Everyone has some kind of fear, no matter how tough that person may appear. Heavyweight boxer Carl "The Truth" Williams had a match scheduled in Japan. Because of his fear of flying, he traveled there by ship. A boxing ring was set up on the ship so he could train for the fight. "I flew as a young pro and a member of the U.S. Boxing team," he explained. "But even then, I had to get drunk to get on the plane."[3]

Here was a man who was afraid to fly but not afraid to fight. Most people would be afraid to fight but not afraid to fly. We are all afraid of something.

What scares you the most? An uncertain future? Losing your health or your job? The economy? Are you being tormented by any of the fears listed below?

- *Fear of the future:* the assumption that disaster will occur

- *Fear of death:* the apprehension about what lies beyond the grave

- *Fear of starvation:* the belief that God will not provide for you

- *Fear of losing your job:* the anxiety that any day the boss will let you go

- *Fear of not getting married:* worrying that God will not bring a spouse to you

- *Fear of rejection:* the phobia that people will not accept you

- *Fear of failure:* the dread that whatever you attempt will end in disappointment

- *Fear of evil:* panicking over possible harm that might come to you or someone you love

Fear makes us nervous, which completely drains us of peace and joy. It forces us to make wrong choices, which keep us from reaching our full potential. As with the man who buried his one talent in the ground (Matthew 25:25), fear will cause us to hide our talents and not take any risks. Playing it safe keeps us from developing the resources God has entrusted to us.

Until we drive fear out of our lives, it will keep steering us into making wrong choices. It will become our master. The fear of being harmed will tell us what we can and cannot do. Faith comes by hearing what God has said (Romans 10:17), but fear comes by listening to what Satan tells us. To kill the giant of fear we must stop listening to its commands.

In the war of the Rhine in 1794, the French took over an Austrian village without striking a blow. Here is how they did it.

Two companies of French foot soldiers were ordered to attack the Austrian village at ten o'clock at night. The six hundred Austrian soldiers who were guarding the city found out about the surprise attack and prepared to defend their village. Communication was to be relayed to the Austrian troops through a trumpeter who would signal when the French attacked.

Little did they know the French had sent their trumpeter, Joseph Werck, under the cover of darkness, to take his position among the Austrian soldiers. At ten o'clock, Werck blew his trumpet for the Austrian soldiers to "rally," and then he sounded "retreat" a few moments later.

Hearing the first trumpet call, the Austrian soldiers quickly rallied together. But then when they heard the second trumpet blast to retreat, they immediately fled from their posts. The French then marched in and captured the village without any opposition.[4]

Just as the Austrians were defeated by listening to the deceptive command of the French trumpet, we can be defeated by following Satan's fearsome orders. Satan cannot overcome the child of God (1 John 4:4), so the only way he can defeat Christians is to intimidate us into running away. Fear is his trumpet sound, commanding us to retreat.

Satan blows his trumpet, and a man loses his confidence and runs away from responsibilities. He blows it again, and an elderly woman can't sleep at night, fearful that a thief will break into her home. He sounds it a third time, and a child is seized with terror. He tries to control everyone in the world with his trumpet. Everyone, that is, who is willing to listen.

Conquering the Giant of Fear

Would you believe me if I told you that it's possible to get rid of all your fears? Permit me to tell you about a person who was 100 percent fear-free. King David said, "I sought the LORD, and He answered me, / And delivered me from all my fears" (Psalm 34:4). If it was possible for him, it's also possible for us. Here are three things you must do that are guaranteed to make fear leave.

1. *Believe that the Lord is with you.*

God told Joshua, "Do not tremble or be dismayed, for the LORD your God is with you wherever you go" (Joshua 1:9). When we are afraid, we want a secure presence with us.

An elderly woman was waiting for a bus in a crime-ridden area when a rookie policeman approached her and asked, "Would you like me to wait with you?"

She answered, "No, thank you. I'm not afraid."

The policeman responded, "Well, I am. Could I wait with you?"

Having someone present with us can be helpful when we're afraid. That's why it's so important to be aware of God's presence. There's something about knowing God is with you that drives away fear. Maybe it's because *fear is afraid of God.*

All throughout Scripture we see the connection between God's presence and fear leaving. David said, "I fear no evil: for thou art with me" (Psalm 23:4 KJV). Moses told Israel, "The LORD is the one who goes ahead of you; He will be with you. He will not fail you or forsake you. Do not fear or be dismayed" (Deuteronomy 31:8). Again the Lord says,

> "Do not fear, for I am with you;
> Do not anxiously look about you, for I am your God.
> I will strengthen you,
> Surely I will uphold you." (Isaiah 41:10)

How many times do we need to read this before it finally sinks in?

Are you ready to do something to get rid of your fear? Here's what you need to do. Simply say out loud, "Lord, I believe that You are with me, so I'm not going to be afraid." Repeat it as many times as you need to, but get it in your heart.

It's so easy to forget this fact when trouble comes. The disciples were on the Sea of Galilee when a violent storm hit. The waves were breaking over the sides so that the boat was filling up with water. Jesus was in the stern, sleeping on a cushion.

The disciples were terrified, thinking they would go under at any moment. They didn't seem to care that the Messiah was in the boat and that His life could also be in danger. They were concerned only about their own safety and survival. They woke Him up and screamed, "Teacher, don't you care that we're going to drown?" (Mark 4:38 NLT).

Even though the Lord was in the boat, their panicking blinded them to the fact that *God was with them.* They didn't realize that Jesus' presence on board was enough to guarantee their own protection. The Father would not allow Jesus to sink to the bottom of the Sea of Galilee when it was predetermined that He would die on the cross for the sins of the world (see Acts 2:23). Jesus was so assured that the Father was in control of the storm that He slept through it.

After the disciples woke Him, Jesus asked, "Why are ye fearful, O ye of little faith?" (Matthew 8:26 KJV). They were "fearful" because of their little faith. Fear had filled the void where their faith should have been.

Faith and fear cannot coexist. We can't be full of fear and full of faith at the same time. We must choose to fill our hearts with faith in God. When we are full of faith, we will have *No Fear*.

Jesus commanded the winds to be still and the sea became perfectly calm, which proved that He was in control of the storm. He had demonstrated to them He was in charge of their circumstances, whether He was sleeping or awake.

The disciples were amazed that He could actually calm the storm simply by speaking words. And He can calm your fears as well by speaking words to your heart. He says to your heart, "Peace, be still. Do not be troubled. Do not be afraid." Listen carefully, and you will hear Him whispering those words to your heart.

You'll never be able to sleep through the storm as Jesus did until you first rest in the fact that God is in control, even when your boat is filling up with water. He's in control of every storm that comes your way. Keep trusting the Lord, even when you don't have your questions answered. God is still with you, even if He appears to be sleeping and unconcerned. It's just a test. The storm will pass, and the boat won't sink. If the Lord doesn't calm the storm you are going through, He will keep you calm through the storm. Either way removes fear.

2. *Face up to what you fear.*

A salesman was making his first visit to see a farmer. He was walking down a long dirt road when he saw a big sign: "Beware of the dog." He paused for a moment and decided to keep going.

As he got farther down the road he saw another sign: "BEWARE OF THE DOG!" He gulped and thought about turning around but decided to proceed. His desire to make the sale was greater than his fears.

Finally, at the end of the road, he arrived at the farmhouse and found a little puppy sitting on the front porch. When the farmer answered the door, the salesman asked, "Do you really expect that little dog to keep people away?"

"No," the farmer replied. "I expect the signs to do that."

Often the thing we dread isn't nearly as bad as we think. It's just a puppy on the porch. What frightens us is when we believe all those scary warning signs along the way. We can't defeat the giant of fear unless we're first willing to face him on the battlefield. Someone once said, "Do the thing you fear, and the death of fear is certain."

I knew a woman who was terrified of flying on an airplane. She had flown a couple of times but never looked out the window because being that high in the air horrified her.

The next time she flew, when she was almost in a state of panic, she decided to do something brave. As she opened her eyes and leaned over to peep out the window, something happened to her when she saw the mountains. Her fear of flying went away!

The majestic view from the perspective of an airplane was something she had never experienced before. She later told me, "I never realized what I had missed all those years by not looking out the window."

She conquered her fear by facing up to it. Fear is like a bully who challenges everyone to fight him. But whenever someone stands up to him, he backs down. The bully of fear tries to scare people away, and the only way to defeat it is to call its bluff.

3. *Trust that God will take care of you.*

Because fear isn't logical, it takes something beyond logic to get rid of it. You can't *think* your way out of being afraid. You can only *trust* your way out of it.

We're usually not afraid of those things that we can control. We're afraid of those things that are out of our hands. That's when we panic.

What can you do about those things that are out of your control? You can place your trust in a God you can't see. You will see Him one day, but it won't be until the day you die. Until that time comes, you must place your confidence in an invisible God to manage the circumstances that are out of your hands.

Placing your trust in God is the only way you'll get rid of your fears. Trust is having confidence in a person, and you can trust an individual only to the degree you understand that person's heart. Jesus spent much of His time communicating to us that He loves us more than we can ever imagine and wants the best for us. He informed us that God "is kind to ungrateful and evil men" (Luke 6:35). If that's how He treats the worst of people, don't you think He wants the best for you?

When King David was going through troubling times, he said,

When I am afraid, I will *put* my trust in You. . . .
In God I have *put* my trust;
I shall not be afraid. (Psalm 56:3–4)

His deliverance came as a direct result of placing his trust in God rather than himself. And we must do the same.

To "put" means to transfer from one place to another. You put gasoline in your car. You put your valuables in a safe-deposit box. So when you put your trust in the Lord, you transfer your confidence to Him.

When I was a kid, I took swimming lessons at the local neighborhood pool. The easy part was when I grabbed on to the side of the pool while someone held me up as I learned how to kick.

Then came the hard part. I had to learn how to float.

It was hard for me to believe that the water would hold me up without any effort of my own. I would try to float, but then my feet would immediately drop down so I could stand up. I didn't fool anyone when I did that awkward "half swim," where I walked along the bottom of the pool while moving my arms like I was swimming.

The instructor kept telling me to trust him—that the water really would hold me up if I would just relax. But that was the problem. I couldn't relax when I thought I was going to drown. In my mind I knew he was right, but in my heart I didn't believe it would work for me.

Then one day, I quit *trying* to float and just went limp. To my surprise, I didn't sink. For the first time in my life I floated, without any effort on my part. When I totally surrendered to the water and quit struggling, it held me up.

That's how we trust God. Inwardly we go limp. We quit struggling and submit to His control. In absolute surrender, we say, "Lord, I'm totally depending on You to come through."

When we put our trust in God, we stop being self-dependent and shift our complete dependency to Him. At the instant we do this, all fears will leave, and we will finally experience peace of mind.

Many times I had read the verse, "You will not be afraid of the terror by night, / Or of the arrow that flies by day" (Psalm 91:5). I didn't really understand that passage until I was placed in a life-threatening situation, and then it finally made sense.

I had gone on an overnight campout at a nearby lake with a couple of elders in our church. Before we left for the lake, we failed to check the weather report.

At sunset we were having a great time of fellowship when we noticed the clouds turning dark. Then the wind suddenly whipped up. Within minutes we were in the middle of a terrible storm. It was pouring buckets, with winds blowing thirty to forty miles per hour. Lightning bolts were striking just a few yards from our tent.

Every few seconds, lightning would strike and thunder would boom around us. I couldn't help but think, *The next one is going to hit us!*

Psalm 91:5 says you will not be afraid of the terror by night. This storm *was* the terror by night—and we were afraid! The small tent where we were huddled together offered zero protection against the lightning bolts striking around us.

I know this sounds crazy, but I actually visualized the headline of our local newspaper: *"Local Pastor and Elders Struck by Lightning,"* see *Obituary page 2*. I really thought that I would never see my family again. I was almost certain that we were all going to die. In all my life, I was never this close to dying.

But then I suddenly remembered the disciples in the boat when the terrible storm hit. We were acting just like the disciples when they woke up Jesus and shouted to Him that they were about to die. At that moment, they didn't believe God was in control of the storm. And now that we were in the same boat, neither did we! We were terrified by the storm instead of trusting in His sovereignty.

I told the other men, "Guys, this is how the disciples must have felt during that storm on the Sea of Galilee, when they went to wake up Jesus. They didn't believe God was in control of the storm, but we know He was because He stopped it. We've got to put our trust in God right now."

We prayed together and told God that we believed He was in control and we trusted Him. As we started praising the Lord, a supernatural peace came over us like a blanket. Words are inadequate to describe how we felt overwhelmed by God's presence. Even though lightning was still striking all around us, the fear instantly vanished, and the storm didn't scare us anymore.

The storm passed. We didn't die. The sun came up. And we learned from experience something we had previously known only in theory: No matter how fierce the storm that comes our way, if we will put our complete trust in God, we will have *No Fear*.

Chapter 3

DISCONTENTMENT

May I Change Seats, Please?

Not that I speak from want, for I have learned to be content in whatever circumstances I am. I know how to get along with humble means, and I also know how to live in prosperity; in any and every circumstance I have learned the secret of being filled and going hungry, both of having abundance and suffering need. (Philippians 4:11–12)

A restlessness that has swept over our country has caused people to lose their happiness. Counselors, despite their best efforts, have not been able to find a cure. I've made up a name for the problem that's causing so many people to be unhappy. I call it Contentment Deficit Disorder. Fortunately, God has the answer for Contentment Deficit Disorder (see next page).

Dr. Jack Hyles told of an experience he once had on a flight from San Francisco to Chicago. He was seated in 4A, and, as he usually did, spoke to the person next to him. "Good morning. How are you today?"

The man did not reply.

Dr. Hyles thought the man might be hard of hearing, so he spoke louder, "Good morning. How are you today?"

> ### *Symptoms of Contentment Deficit Disorder*
>
> Lack of commitment to other people
>
> Compulsion to move away to another city
>
> Extremely strong desire to quit your job
>
> Urgency to leave your spouse
>
> Desire to drop out of school
>
> Restlessness compelling you to run from your present circumstances
>
> Attitude that anything is better than what you have right now

Once again the man didn't acknowledge him. Dr. Hyles knew right then he was seated next to a crab, that is, a very difficult person.

The flight attendant came by and took the man's order for breakfast. The man spoke to her but wouldn't speak to him.

He asked, "Where are you going?" He knew that was a dumb question because everyone on the plane was going to Chicago.

The man didn't respond.

Dr. Hyles thought, *This old crab is ruining my trip. I have to sit next to him for four more hours. He is not going to ruin my trip.*

He called the flight attendant and asked, "Ma'am, may I change seats please?"

She said, "I'm sorry, but the plane is full. You must stay in your assigned seat."

He looked at the man and said, "If you think you're going to ruin my trip, you're mistaken." The man never looked up.[1]

All of us are on a plane ride, heading toward a destination. To enjoy the trip, you must understand a couple of things. First, God has assigned you a seat in life. Second, you are probably going to be seated next to a crab.

That crab may be a difficult person with whom you work. It may be your spouse, a relative, a next-door neighbor, or maybe even some difficult circumstances you are going through. And that crab is ruining your trip.

So you cry out to God praying, "May I change seats, please? Can I move away from this situation?"

He answers, "No, this is your assigned seat in life. Buckle your seat belt and enjoy the trip!"

Five Secrets of Finding Happiness

How do you enjoy the trip through life when you're seated next to a crab? Here are five secrets to finding happiness.

Secret 1: *Accept the fact that God has given you an assigned seat.*

A lot of seats we would never choose on our own, but God has assigned them to us. Paul wrote Philippians from a Roman prison. The prisons in biblical times were different from today's penitentiaries. Paul didn't have cable TV or a recreation room to lift weights. He didn't have air-conditioning, heating, health and dental care, or three meals a day. No, he was bound by chains without the entertainment features many prisoners have today.

If given a choice, Paul would not have chosen to go to prison for preaching the gospel. He would have preferred to be preaching on the streets or on a missionary journey. But his assigned seat at that time was not on the streets or on a ship. It was in a Roman prison.

So what did Paul do? He learned to accept his assigned seat. He didn't understand why God would allow him to be arrested, but, rather than complaining about it, he learned to be content in prison.

He didn't realize that the letter he was writing in jail about the secret of contentment would be included in the Bible and bring encouragement to hundreds of millions of people in future generations. God doesn't always reveal to us what He's up to, so that's why we must trust Him rather than making an evaluation on what we see right now.

Have you learned to be happy in your present situation? Have you accepted the seat that God has assigned you? Until you do, you will always be asking Him to let you change seats.

I knew a man who had been married for ten years to his wife, and they had three children. The family moved forty times in those ten years. That's four times a year, once every three months.

Why did he move his family so much? He had Contentment Deficit Disorder. He moved from job to job and state to state, always looking for that perfect place where he could be happy. But there was one place he forgot to look. He didn't look inside his own heart. God had assigned him a seat in life, but he didn't want to sit in it.

Secret 2: *Learn to get along with your troublemaker.*

Paul said he had learned how to get along in both poverty and prosperity. He discovered the secret of being filled and going hungry, of having abundance and suffering need.

I'm sure Paul was seated next to some crabs in prison. Thieves and murderers were in there. Probably some perverts too. No doubt some people hated him because of his preaching to them about Jesus. Others had obnoxious personalities that rubbed him the wrong way. They probably stank, since they had no deodorant or fabric softener to make their clothes smell fresh. No mints for their bad breath either. These were the crabs Paul learned to coexist with, and he wasn't going to let them steal his happiness.

The grizzly bear is the meanest animal in the forest. It can end the life of any other creature with one swipe of its paw. But there's one animal that the grizzly bear will not attack. He has even allowed this animal to eat with him, although it is his adversary.

The animal I am talking about is the skunk. The grizzly bear does not like the skunk, but he has decided it's better to coexist with him than to create a stink. Sometimes it's better to learn how to get along with the difficult person in your life than fight him and make your situation even worse.

If your problem is a coworker, or maybe your boss, it's better to get along with that person than to quit your job. Many people get irritated by the nuisance they work with and, in a moment of frustration, quit their jobs. They end up hurting themselves more than they hurt the other person. It's better to tolerate the situation than to be out of work and have no income.

God has a purpose for the crab in your life. That's why He assigned you a seat next to him. God is using him to teach you a few things. One of those things is how to love crabs! It's easy to love the lovely, but Jesus wants us to love our enemies. He said, "If you love those who love you, what credit is that to you? For even sinners love those who love them" (Luke 6:32).

A man was working a crossword puzzle and asked, "What is a four-letter word for a strong emotional reaction toward a difficult person?"

Someone standing nearby said, "The answer is hate."

A woman interrupted and said, "No, the answer is love."

Everyone is working that same crossword puzzle, but the way you answer is up to you.

Secret 3: *Realize that changing seats doesn't solve your problem.*

Some people live in Never Never Land; they're never happy, and they're never satisfied. They think, *If I could just change seats, then I'll be happy. If I can just run away and find a new set of circumstances, then I will finally find happiness.* That assumption simply isn't true. Let's examine a few myths about seat changing.

Myth 1: If I could be with someone else, then I would be happy.

Discontented people think that if they could just be with someone else, then their problems would be over. But that won't work, because discontentment is an internal not an external problem. Yet many people have never figured this out. They are consumed with changing seats, because it's easier to change seats than it is to deal with your crab.

Single people want to change seats and get married; married people want to change seats and be single again. Like flies on a screen door, the flies on the inside want to get out, and the flies on the outside want to get in.

The grass always looks greener on the other side of the fence. That's because it's artificial turf. It is only an illusion. People with Contentment

Deficit Disorder (CDD) spend their lives chasing illusions that are always just beyond their reach.

A man in the desert was dying of thirst and saw a lemonade stand on the next sand dune. He ran to it, but when he arrived, the lemonade stand disappeared and reappeared on the next sand dune. When he ran to the next and grabbed for the lemonade, it disappeared and reappeared again on the next dune. He continued to chase it from dune to dune until he died of thirst. He was chasing a mirage—just an illusion in his mind.

We must make a distinction between what's real and what's a pipe dream. Those with CDD convince themselves that fantasy is reality and will exchange whatever they have for whatever they perceive to be better.

A dog with a bone in his mouth was crossing over a bridge. He looked over the edge and saw his reflection in the water. Not realizing that he was looking at a mirror image, he coveted the bone in the other dog's mouth. When he opened his mouth to grab for the other dog's bone, he dropped the bone into the stream. He gave up what he owned for something that didn't exist.

Some discontented people will leave their spouses for what they think will be an exciting new life with someone else. They soon discover that the infatuation quickly wears off, just as it did with the previous partner. The following letter was written to Ann Landers:

Dear Ann:

Sometimes you feel lonely and unloved in a marriage, even after 23 years. You feel as if there's got to be more to life, so you set out to find someone who can make you blissfully happy. You believe you have found that someone and decide he is exactly what you want. So you pack up and say good-bye to your 23-year marriage and all the friends you made when you were part of the couple.

You live the glorious life for a few years, and then, a light bulb goes on in your empty head. You realize that you have exactly the same life you had before. The only difference is that you've lost your friends, your children's respect, and the best friend you loved and shared everything with for 23 years. And you miss him. You cannot undo what has been done, so you settle for a lonely and loveless life with emptiness in your heart.

Ann, please print my letter so others won't give up something that is truly precious—and let them know that they won't know how precious it is until they have thrown it away.

Heavyhearted in Philly[2]

Myth 2: If I could just go somewhere else, then I would be happy.

It's tempting to think that if you'll escape to somewhere else, all your problems will be solved. But it doesn't work that way because everywhere you go, there you are! You take *you* with you. If you are currently unhappy, you'll take the same situation to a new location.

Several years ago my friend Phil interviewed for a job in Wichita, Kansas. After thoroughly researching the situation, he wasn't sure what to do. He was tired of his job and wanted to move away, but something didn't seem right about this new place of employment. He suspected some possible problems, so he reluctantly withdrew his name from consideration and remained at his job.

For the next two years, Phil kicked himself for turning down the job. Every time something went wrong at his workplace, he thought about how happy he would have been if he had taken the position in Wichita.

One day he boarded a plane and a businessman sat down next to him. Phil asked him what he did for a living. The man explained that he had taken a job two years earlier in Wichita but absolutely hated it. Every day he had to deal with trouble and conflict in the office. As he continued to give more details, Phil realized that this man had accepted the position at the company where he had applied two years earlier!

Phil was stunned. For two years he believed he had made the wrong decision by turning down the job. Instead, he discovered that God actually protected him from almost making a horrible mistake.[3] The Lord had arranged this meeting to reveal the agony he would have experienced if he had accepted the job.

My mother grew up always dreaming of living in a house on the beach. She said it would be wonderful to sit on the beach, watching the sun set over the water. After she was married to my father, they moved to a little cottage on the beach, fulfilling her lifelong dream. But things turned out differently than she had thought.

The tourists walking in front of their house were a nuisance. She didn't like the humidity because it made her feel sticky. Sand found its way into the bed, on the couch, and into the sandwiches they ate. After a while, she quit looking at the sunsets. My mom said she was glad when they moved away.

No matter where you move, sooner or later you'll discover problems in your new situation that you weren't aware of before. No place is problem-free, no matter how perfectly it may have been portrayed before you got there.

Of course that doesn't mean God never wants you to move. He will probably lead you to many new situations. But always keep in mind that the grass is never quite as green once you get to the other side. And it's hard to see those weeds from a distance. When you change seats, you'll have a different set of problems to deal with.

Myth 3: If I could just have one more thing, then I would be happy.

Contentment is not having everything you want, but wanting everything you have. God has supplied us with all things to enjoy (see 1 Timothy 6:17), but our hearts must be right before we can enjoy them. If you aren't happy with the things you already have, you won't be happy with the new things you receive.

A beggar standing on a street corner told his friends, "If I only had a hundred dollars, I would never complain again."

A businessman walking by overheard his comment and said, "Did you say if you only had a hundred dollars, you would never complain again?"

"You heard right, mister," the beggar replied.

The man handed him a hundred dollars and said, "I'm glad I can bring a little bit of happiness to the world."

After the man walked away, the beggar turned to his friends and said, "Now I wish I had asked for $200!"

When you are discontented, you will never be satisfied, because "enough" is never enough. Did it ever occur to you that the things you now have were once things that you were desperately trying to get? But after you acquired the item, it wasn't long before you didn't notice it anymore. The luster wore off and you started pursuing something else. That's why discontented people don't need to change seats; they need to change their hearts.

Secret 4: *Play the cards that have been dealt to you.*

Life isn't fair, and the sooner you accept that fact, the quicker you'll find contentment. If you expect life to be fair, you'll always be angry. That's why Paul said in effect, "I've learned to accept the fact that life isn't fair, and that's okay. I'm serving God, not my circumstances. I have learned to play the cards that have been dealt to me."

When playing a card game, everyone is dealt a different hand, and each person must play those particular cards. In the game of life, everybody is playing a different set of cards. Some people hold good cards, while others have been dealt bad hands.

Perhaps you were laid off from your job. Maybe you've been through a painful divorce or were hurt in an accident. You're upset because other players always seem to have the good cards, or maybe they're winning because they've been cheating. Although you've been dealt a bad hand, you still need to play your cards. The game isn't over, despite the crooked dealers and stacked decks.

You may not be responsible for the hand you hold, but you are responsible for the way you play those cards. Stop complaining about your bad hand and keep playing, trusting the Lord in spite of what you see right now. The secret to contentment is to cheerfully work through your circumstances and trust God for the outcome. He promises to give each believer a winning hand in the end. "We know that God causes all things to work together for good to those who love God, to those who are called according to His purpose" (Romans 8:28).

Secret 5: *Choose to be happy in your current situation.*

Contentment in life isn't found in a perfect set of circumstances, but by *choosing to be happy in every situation*. It's a decision that you make in your heart.

Paul was an inmate in prison, but he didn't let that small matter take away his happiness. They could imprison his body, but they couldn't imprison his thankful spirit. He thanked God for the free room and board and seized the opportunity to witness to the Roman guards. He wrote letters in prison that are now in the Bible. Paul always made lemonade in every situation he was in.

A husband and wife enjoyed playing the here's-how-I-would-remodel-that-house game as they traveled. They took turns picking out certain houses along the highway and explained how they would remodel the home. They saw an old, dilapidated house that looked like it had been abandoned. The husband stopped out front and said, "I tell you what I'd do with that shack. I'd bulldoze it down and start over."

At that moment, an elderly man stepped out of the house on to the front porch. With a big smile on his face, the old man waved at them as though they were long-lost friends. The couple waved back and then drove on down the road.

The husband asked, "Do you think he would have been that friendly if he knew what I said about his house?"

After a long pause the wife replied, "Probably so!"

The happiest people in the world are those who don't allow anything or anyone to steal their joy. When you stop placing conditions on your happiness, you've learned the secret of being content.

Too many people are so fixated on annoying people and unpleasant circumstances that they can't enjoy life. God wants you to enjoy your journey through this life, but to do that you cannot let the crab ruin your trip.

Make up your mind right now, "Crabby person, you are not going to ruin my trip! Difficult situation, you're not going to force me to change seats! Lord, I'm going to be happy in my current situation and rejoice in it, no matter how difficult it may be."

DISCONTENTMENT

Don't get the idea that contentment means God will never lead you to a new place. More than likely, He will lead you to make quite a few changes during your lifetime. He just doesn't want discontentment to drive you into a situation that's out of His will.

If God lets you change seats, just remember that another crab will want to sit next to you. It's part of the cure for Contentment Deficit Disorder.

Chapter 4

DOUBT

Without a Doubt

Now when John, while imprisoned, heard of the works of Christ, he sent word by his disciples, and said to Him, "Are You the Expected One, or shall we look for someone else?" Jesus answered and said to them, "Go and report to John what you hear and see: the blind receive sight and the lame walk, the lepers are cleansed and the deaf hear, and the dead are raised up, and the poor have the gospel preached to them. And blessed is he who keeps from stumbling over Me." (Matthew 11:2–6)

He used to be so confident. Now, he wasn't so sure.

Many would say John the Baptist was at his lowest point in his ministry. At one time, depending upon your viewpoint, he was the most famous or infamous person in Israel. His preaching had swayed the multitudes.

But now things were different. Most of his disciples were following Jesus. His popularity had dwindled. John himself had said, "He must increase, but I must decrease" (John 3:30). But decrease this far? He had no idea he would hit bottom in a dark dungeon.

It's enough to make a guy start wondering. Maybe even doubt.

Doubts about his calling. Doubts about the faithfulness of God. Even doubts about the man he had been bragging about. Jesus.

John asked himself, *Is He really the Messiah? Or did I make one gigantic blunder when I told everyone that He's the one we've been waiting for?* He decided to send word to Jesus through his disciples to get his questions answered.

Dear Jesus,

I am writing to inform you that I have been thrown into prison by Herod. I've had a lot of time to think since I have been here. I've been thinking about all of those things that I had preached about you, even before you began your ministry.

Remember how I told everyone that your winnowing fork was in your hand, and you would thoroughly clean your threshing floor? And remember how I said you would burn up the chaff with unquenchable fire? To me that meant that you would put an end to all injustice. I was counting on you to correct all wrongs.

To be quite honest with you, Jesus, I never thought I'd have to write a note like this. Things haven't worked out like I thought they would. I was sure you would have straightened things up around here by now. Rumors have it that Herodias wants my head. If you are wondering when to get out your winnowing fork to start cleaning up, now would be a pretty good time. That is, if you are the one we are expecting.

Respectfully yours,
John the Baptist

P.S. If we are to look for someone else, please let us know.

A few days later, the mailman delivered a letter to John's jail cell. He eagerly opened it, hoping to receive news that Jesus was arranging for his quick release from prison. Instead, John read this reply:

Dear John the Baptist,

The blind receive sight, the lame walk, the lepers are cleansed, the deaf hear, the dead are raised, the poor have the gospel preached to them.

Agape,
Jesus

P.S. Blessed is he who keeps from stumbling over me.

We expect doubters to become believers. But not for believers to become doubters. That's a little bit hard to swallow. Especially when you're talking about John the Baptist. We might expect Thomas to doubt. The guy was one big question mark. But John the Baptist? This man was an exclamation point! His whole ministry was filled with courage and confidence, being the first one to boldly proclaim that Jesus was the Lamb of God who takes away the sin of the world.

Remember the time when John called the Pharisees and Sadducees a brood of vipers? Boy, were they mad at him that day. He didn't so much as blink in response to them. John didn't have a smidgen of a doubt he was right. And you should have seen him when he told Herod it was unlawful to have his brother's wife. He had the king sweating bullets. Not an inkling of a doubt there either.

If you take a look at a résumé of John's life, it reads like a *Who's Who of Nondoubters.*

Résumé of John the Baptist

Name: John (the Baptist). Named by the angel Gabriel, who appeared to my dad in the temple and told him what to name me (Luke 1:13–19).

Birth: Miraculous. My mother was far too old to have children, but God made sure she got pregnant with me (Luke 1:7).

Prophet Qualifications

- Filled with the Holy Spirit in my mother's womb (Luke 1:15).

- Forerunner before Messiah in the spirit and power of Elijah (Luke 1:17).

- Fulfilled prophecies in the Old Testament (Isaiah 40:3; Malachi 4:5–6).

Ministry Experience

- Baptized Jesus in the Jordan River.

- Saw heavens opened and the Spirit descending upon Jesus as a dove.

- Heard a voice from heaven say, "This is My beloved Son, in whom I am well pleased."

- Preached to the multitudes. Started with no disciples but grew my congregation to thousands.

Other Comments: Willing to live on a meager salary. Cheap to clothe and feed. I own one camel's hair garment. I eat locusts and wild honey.

How could this bulldozer, who cleared the road for the Messiah, now be wavering on his beliefs? Many of us wrongly assume all the great men of faith in the Bible never had any doubts, but we find that was not the case.

David, a man after God's heart, was plagued with doubts. He wrote, "How long, O LORD? Will You forget me forever? / How long will You hide Your face from me?" (Psalm 13:1).

The great prophet Elijah also faltered in his faith. After Elijah defeated the 850 false prophets of Baal and Asherah on Mount Carmel, King Ahab's wife, Jezebel, threatened to kill him. Elijah ran like a scared rabbit because he thought God wouldn't protect him.

God told the prophet Jonah to go preach to the cruel people in Nineveh, who were known to poke out the eyes of their enemies. He ran away in the opposite direction and hid on a ship going to Tarshish.

How about the prophet Jeremiah? Yep, even Jerry dabbled in doubt. When people rejected his message, he wondered why God would allow such a thing. He thought the Lord had purposely deceived him (Jeremiah 20:7).

And of course we all know Thomas doubted that Jesus rose from the dead. But how many of us remember that *all* the disciples refused to believe He rose from the dead (Mark 16:11, 14)?

What exactly is doubt? Doubt is not unbelief, but it's not faith either. It wavers between faith and unbelief, unable to make up its mind which one it wants to be. It's like the hitchhiker who was thumbing a ride with his hand in one direction—and thumbing a ride with his other hand in the opposite direction. He wasn't sure which way he wanted to go.

James tells us that doubt is being double-minded, which makes a person unstable in all his ways.

> But he must ask in faith without any doubting, for the one who doubts is like the surf of the sea, driven and tossed by the wind. For that man ought not to expect that he will receive anything from the Lord, being a double-minded man, unstable in all his ways. (James 1:6–8)

A person controlled by doubt is unsure how to think straight. Here are some of the characteristics of doubt.

A person who doubts is . . .

Tossed up and down emotionally.

He is tossed around like the surf of the sea. If you have ever been on the sea in a boat, the waves will take you up, then down. Up, then down. When you doubt, you are controlled by your ups and downs. One minute you're up emotionally, and the next minute you're down emotionally. You can't take this very long without becoming seasick.

Thrown back and forth doctrinally.

James 1:6 says the one who doubts is driven by the wind. You're being pushed around by outside forces instead of being guided by faith. Ephesians 4:14 says the one who is weak in faith will be thrown back and forth by every wind of doctrine. The doubter is unsure of what to really believe, because he can't discern between truth and error.

Torn between yes and no mentally.

Doubt is having two minds inside you. A double-minded person says yes at first, and then a little while later changes the answer to no.

Scientists once studied a snake that was double-minded. It was born with two heads. Each head had a mind of its own which would try to control the body. One moment it would crawl one way, then the other mind would take over, and the snake would crawl in a completely different direction. It truly was double-minded.

That's the picture of the one who doubts. As confused as a termite inside a yo-yo, he doesn't know which way is up and which way is down. He is lacking direction, always looking back on past decisions and wondering if he has made a mistake.

We have all had to fight this giant. Doubt makes us wonder what to do next. We're not sure what to believe. We have second thoughts about the decisions we've made in the past, which makes us even more uncertain about the decisions we need to make for the future.

That's why John doubted. He had paved the highway for the Messiah to journey on, but now he was locked up in prison while Jesus traveled down the road without him. Jesus didn't seem to appreciate all the work John had done for Him. The least a Messiah could do would be to visit him in prison, which was what Jesus told His disciples to do (see Matthew 25:36).

What John had said about Jesus being a Great Deliverer seemed to be nothing more than a Great Disappointment. Jesus appeared to be unconcerned that John was about to have his head chopped off. How could He be so uncaring? In John's mind, everything he had preached about justice and righteousness was now in question.

The Two Shall Become One

We start doubting when what we expect to happen *isn't* happening, or what shouldn't be happening *is* happening. Circumstances appear to be in conflict about what we should believe, which throws us into confusion. As a result, we waver between the two, wondering which is right.

Doubt is having two minds instead of one. Is there any way to turn a double mind into a single mind? Here are some ways to grow your faith and shrink your doubts.

1. *Question your doubts, not your faith.*

Instead of questioning your faith, question your doubts. That's what John the Baptist did. Instead of letting his doubts continue to push him around, he faced them head on. He knew truth would stand up for itself because it can pass the test of scrutiny.

So John packed up his doubts and sent them to Jesus. The answer Jesus sent back revealed John needed to make some adjustments in his beliefs. John had been preaching about Jesus, quoting from Isaiah concerning the Messiah's *second* coming. When Jesus sent word back to John, he quoted verses from Isaiah concerning His *first* coming. John was confused because he had the right person, but the wrong timing. Many times we doubt because a piece of the puzzle is missing, and once we see what it is, everything makes sense.

John wasn't wrong in what he believed about Jesus, but he needed to make some adjustments in his theology. Doubts can be a stepping stone, rather than a stumbling block, if we will allow them to expose weak points in our belief system so we can correct them.

We are all growing in our understanding of God. Apollos was a man who understood the Scriptures and was enthusiastically teaching others about Jesus. But Priscilla and Aquila knew that he needed more information, so they took him aside and explained the way of God to him "more accurately" (see Acts 18:24–26). Faith grows and doubts diminish whenever we adjust our beliefs to line up more accurately with God's Word.

2. *Concentrate on what you know, not on what you don't know.*

We will always have questions that can't be answered. Doubts creep in when we think about things we don't know the answers to. When we dwell on the unanswered question, it grows in our minds and becomes a giant more powerful than the things we know for certain. Jesus responded to John's question by getting him to recall the facts he knew to be true.

"John, I have opened blind eyes. That's a miracle no one else has ever done. Remember, John, the prophet Isaiah predicted that the Messiah would do this (see Isaiah 29:18; 35:5; 42:7). I've healed people who were paralyzed and have cleansed lepers. I've made the deaf to hear and even raised people from the dead. I've preached the gospel to the poor and not just the wealthy. Now, John, you know I did these miracles.

Who else can do these things, except the Messiah? If you will concentrate on these facts, your doubts will disappear."

After Jesus healed a man's blindness, the Pharisees questioned the former blind man as to whether or not Jesus was a sinner. He answered, "Whether He is a sinner, I do not know; *one thing I do know*, that though I was blind, now I see" (John 9:25). He concentrated on the fact he knew to be true, not on the question he didn't know.

You also know many things that are true. "Finally, brethren, whatever is true . . . dwell on these things" (Philippians 4:8). Satan will attack your mind with lies and confusing thoughts, but you don't have to take the bait. You get to choose what you think about. This passage says to focus your thoughts on the truth.

We know God's Word is true through Bible prophecies that have been fulfilled. Because God knows the future, He was able to tell His prophets specific events that would happen, which they recorded in the Scriptures. Hundreds of those prophecies came to pass, which verifies that the Bible can be trusted.

Jesus fulfilled more than three hundred prophecies during His life on earth. Many Old Testament prophecies concerning other things also came to pass. Since the Scriptures have accurately predicted numerous future events, we know that it's telling us the truth on everything else. Place your faith in these facts rather than dwelling on the questions that can't be answered.

You may recall when God answered a prayer that can't be explained through logic. Perhaps He spoke to you clearly or did something miraculous in your life. Perhaps you've had a "divine appointment" where people and circumstances came together at just the right moment—and you know that it didn't happen by accident. He might have touched you in a special way, and you knew it was God who did it. Recalling these facts rather than dwelling on confusion will help defeat doubt.

3. *Trust in the Lord with your heart, not your head.*

All doubt is "reasonable doubt." It always tries to figure out the reasons why God's plan won't work. Doubt disables us when it comes to making a decision. We can't make up our minds, because we have so many questions. God wants to guide us in the decision-making process, but it requires that we put our trust in Him. That sounds easy, but the difficulty arises when He instructs us in ways that go against our logic.

God knows things that we don't. He sees the outcome of every choice down the road. He's aware of future factors that aren't observable in our present situations. That's why He tells us to trust Him with our entire hearts and to not depend on our limited, human logic in making decisions. "Trust in the LORD with all your heart / And do not lean on your own understanding" (Proverbs 3:5).

Trust comes from believing that our Father knows what's best for us in the long run. When we are totally submitted to Him, He will place a peaceful "inner knowing" in our hearts that points us in the right direction, even if it does not make sense at the time. At this crucial time we must trust Him with all our hearts and not depend on our abilities to figure it out.

Inside every airplane are instruments that are critical to flying the aircraft. The instruments will give a true and accurate reading of how the aircraft is flying, even if a pilot thinks otherwise. On a clear, sunny day, a pilot may not need to look at some of these instruments, but at night or in poor visibility these instruments become vital to the pilot's survival. Many planes have crashed because the pilot became disoriented and trusted his own sense of direction instead of his instruments.

While attending Texas A&M University, Jeff Patton and I became friends as members of the Corps of Cadets. He is now Col. Jeff Patton and flew as an F-15 fighter pilot in the first Gulf War. On the first night of the war, his mission was to escort a large formation of fighters in bombing a chemical weapons plant in northern Iraq. The date for the attack was chosen because the absence of moonlight and the high clouds helped prevent the enemy defenses from detecting the Allied fighters. Flying in total darkness, the pilots were completely dependent on their instruments.

Shortly after crossing into Iraq, an Iraqi surface-to-air-missile radar locked on to Jeff's plane. He erratically maneuvered his aircraft to break the radar's lock on him. He successfully broke the lock, but it created a different problem. Those radical movements in the dark gave him vertigo, which made him disoriented. He couldn't tell which way was up or down.

His mind was telling him his plane was in a climbing right turn, but his instruments indicated he was in a 60-degree dive toward the ground! He felt certain that he was climbing instead of diving, and his mind was screaming at him to lower the nose of his F-15 to halt the climb.

Now he had to make a decision—and his life depended on making the right one. Should he trust his own senses or his instruments? His mind told him to correct the plane by turning it downward, but his instruments instructed him to do just the opposite. Because he was flying in total darkness, he had to decide quickly. The wrong decision could mean death.

In flight training he had been drilled many times to trust his instruments in situations like this. It took everything within him to overcome what his mind was telling him, but he decided to ignore his senses and maneuver his plane upward. He rolled his wings level and pulled his F-15 upward, which drew seven times the force of gravity, pulling the aircraft out of its dive. It only took a few moments to realize he had made the right decision. If he had lowered the nose of his jet, as his mind had been telling him, he would have crashed the plane. Trusting his instruments saved his life.

Immediately he looked at his altimeter, which told him the elevation of his aircraft. He had narrowly escaped colliding into the mountains of Iraq by just two thousand feet. He realized if he had delayed just three more seconds, his plane would have crashed into the mountains. Even right decisions can be wrong ones if they are made too late.

God will guide our hearts through the "instruments" of His Word and His Spirit, even though logic may be telling us to do something else. We can't keep vacillating between God's instructions and what we think is right. Just as pilots are drilled to trust their instruments, we must place our trust in God's spiritual instruments to point us in the right direction.

When you place your trust in the Lord rather than your own understanding, your doubts will disappear. But don't take too much time trying to decide. If you don't make up your mind now, you'll probably regret it later.

Chapter 5

TEMPTATION

Adam and Eve's Instruction Manual

Now the serpent was more crafty than any beast of the field which the LORD God had made. And he said to the woman, "Indeed, has God said, 'You shall not eat from any tree of the garden'?" And the woman said to the serpent, "From the fruit of the trees of the garden we may eat; but from the fruit of the tree which is in the middle of the garden, God has said, 'You shall not eat from it or touch it, or you will die.'" And the serpent said to the woman, "You surely shall not die! . . ." When the woman saw that the tree was good for food, and that it was a delight to the eyes, and that the tree was desirable to make one wise, she took from its fruit and ate; and she gave also to her husband with her, and he ate. (Genesis 3:1–4, 6)

> August 22, 2063 A.D. (Global News Network)
> Archaeologists digging in the Middle East uncovered a tablet last month that has sent shock waves across the world. Translators have been able to decipher what appears to be a list of instructions left by the first two humans on earth. The artifact reads "Adam and Eve's Instruction Manual for Reducing Temptations." The ancient document contains a list of lessons they passed on to the future human race, explaining how to overcome temptation. It is signed by "Adam and Eve."

Of course no such document has ever been found. But let's suppose it had been discovered. What would Adam and Eve tell us about how to overcome temptation? They could give us a step-by-step document explaining how they were tempted and how others could avoid it.

Temptation hasn't changed much since the first one. The tactics are the same. The principles involved are identical. The only thing that has changed is the bait. Our forbidden fruit may not be hanging on a tree, but it is still off limits. Here is a list of the lessons Adam and Eve would teach us from what they learned in the garden.

Eight Lessons from Adam and Eve

Lesson 1: *You can reduce your temptations by avoiding the places of temptation.*

Have you ever wondered why God put the forbidden tree in the middle of the garden? That was no accident. He could have planted it anywhere, but God chose that spot because He wanted Adam and Eve to know exactly where it was *so they could avoid it.* It is always easier to avoid temptation than to overcome it. If they could avoid that place, they wouldn't be tempted. They knew exactly where the forbidden tree was located, so they could stay away from it and enjoy the rest of the garden.

A man broke his arm and went to see the doctor. He walked in, clutching his arm in great pain. "Doc, you gotta help me," he moaned. "I broke my arm in two places. What should I do?"

The doctor said, "There's only one thing you can do. Stay away from those places."

We get hurt many times because we go to the wrong places. Staying away from those places can keep us from getting into trouble.

Temptations usually begin with a thought to go to a certain place. The temptation began for Adam and Eve when they decided to take a trip to the middle of the garden. The Tree of Life was also in the middle of the garden, but that's not why they went there. They went there to examine the wrong tree. When they chose to inspect forbidden fruit, they entered into temptation.

Temptation always covers an area that can be entered into. Once we have crossed that invisible line to go into the forbidden area, we've entered into temptation.

Every boxing ring has rope around the area where the boxers fight. If you stay outside the ring, you will be safe. But once you enter into the ring, temptation will begin to fight with you.

I once counseled a man who had a drinking problem. After he left his job every day, he would stop at the bar on his way home. When I asked him where the bar was located, he told me it was on the direct route between his job and his house. I explained to him that when he drove past the bar, he had entered into temptation. So I rerouted him home from work on different streets where he wouldn't have the option of stopping at the bar. He later told me that avoiding the bar was an important factor in overcoming his temptation to drink.

Jesus taught us to pray, "Lead us not into temptation" (Luke 11:4). This doesn't mean that God leads us into temptation and we must beg Him to stop doing it. It means God can lead us in such a way that we will avoid the areas of temptation. That's why Jesus said, "Keep watching and praying that you may not *enter into* temptation" (Matthew 26:41). This is a pre-temptation instruction. Watching and praying can keep us from entering into those areas where we will be tempted.

Lesson 2: *The door of temptation opens when you decide you want to be tempted.*

Have you ever wanted to be tempted? You're cracking open a dangerous door, which is an attempt to provide for your desires in the wrong way. God says, "Make no provision for the flesh in regard to its lusts" (Romans 13:14). A person starts being tempted "when he is carried away and enticed by his own lust" (James 1:14). That selfish part of you called "the flesh" will escort you to the wrong places.

Provision means "to foresee." People who want to be tempted will look ahead and plan to be in a place where they can provide for their flesh. It's hard to be victorious over temptation when you also want to be overcome by it.

One day Bobby's mother told him not to go swimming in the pond when he came home from school. Bobby told her he wouldn't but took along his bathing suit—just in case he was tempted. By thinking ahead and making plans to disobey, he made provision for the flesh.

My favorite ice cream flavor is vanilla bean. When I am being tempted by this delicacy, my taste buds become stronger than my mind, will, and emotions. If a carton of vanilla bean had been hanging on the tree in the garden, I would have been first in line with my spoon. Forget the fact it may not have one ounce of nutrition; my flesh loves this stuff.

If I see an ice cream commercial on television, my taste buds dance. My salivary glands burst with excitement. I start craving ice cream.

This is followed by a conversation inside my head, "Kent, you don't drink, do drugs, smoke, or chew. You're in pretty good health, and you deserve a break. You've been working hard lately. Reward yourself with a little ice cream."

Within moments I have the car keys in hand and tell my wife, "Honey, I'm going to run to the grocery store for a few things and will be back in a little bit."

I don't fool her for one second. She knows that once I've decided to go to the store, I will provide for my ice cream craving.

Adam and Eve did the same thing when they made a decision to go to the middle of the garden. God had said, "From the tree of the knowledge of good and evil you shall not eat, for in the day that you eat from it you will surely die" (Genesis 2:17). An invisible line was drawn in the dirt around the tree, marking off the area where they would fall into temptation.

They were some distance away from the forbidden tree when one of them said, "I guess it wouldn't hurt anything just to take a look at it."

"Yeah, I'm a little curious about it myself," the other one said.

In that defining moment, they cracked open the door that would eventually bring down humanity. They made provision for their flesh by deciding to take a closer look at the forbidden tree.

Lesson 3: *When you get to the place of temptation, Satan will be waiting there for you.*

When Adam and Eve arrived at the middle of the garden, guess who just happened to be waiting at the tree? Satan! How did he know to be waiting for them at that spot? He knew that was the place where they could be tempted. Satan can tempt us easier in some places than others. He likes to hang around the places of temptation.

Not only are we to make *no provision* for the flesh, but we are also to make *no place* for the devil (see Ephesians 4:27 KJV). When I make a place in my mind for Satan to fill, I have made a place for the devil. He first gets me to think about eating vanilla bean. If he can get me to think about eating ice cream while I am standing in the frozen foods section of the store, I'm in double trouble. (By now you've figured out that vanilla bean ice cream represents every temptation.)

After I've cracked open the door of my mind, Satan sticks his foot in the door. If he can get a foothold, then he can make a stronghold. The devil knows that once I make a place in my mind to provide for the flesh, he can pour in suggestions concerning the temptation. Now I've given him permission to speak lying thoughts to my mind, which will seem to make sense.

Not every thought that pops into your mind comes from you. You can also receive thoughts from God and Satan. The ideas that pull you toward the temptation come from the enemy, while the ideas to keep you in freedom come from the Lord.

So now we see a couple of things that are involved in temptation. We struggle with the flesh on the inside and Satan on the outside. When we make provision for the flesh and a place for the devil, we become extremely vulnerable to yielding to the temptation.

Lesson 4: *Once you are "under the influence" of temptation, you'll become blind to the consequences.*

Outside of the area of temptation, we can easily see the consequences of what can happen to us if we yield. But after we have entered into temptation, we get "under the influence" and become blind to the danger. Temptations don't usually look like temptations, especially when we have been observing them for a while. When Eve entered into temptation, she failed to recognize it as such.

This tree doesn't look too harmful, she thought. *It seems to have a lot of good points. It's good for food. It delights me to look at it, and I've been told it will increase my wisdom. I don't see any consequences if I eat from it.*

51

It's no secret that ice cream is a delight to the taste buds and has the ability to make one fat. After I go to the grocery store, I only remember the delight-to-the–taste-buds part. The "ability to make one fat" applies only to other people, not me.

Sometimes the nutrition label listing the calories and grams of fat can deter me from buying a food item. But once I have decided to buy vanilla bean, the nutrition label means nothing. "Let's see: 350 calories per cup, 10 grams of fat." This last warning doesn't even faze me. I divert my eyes from the nutrition label to the ingredients. I tell myself, *The milk products listed in the ingredients will be good for me. This isn't that bad.*

After I've entered into temptation, I ignore all warning signs. By now I'm totally blind to the consequences. The truth is, the result of delighting my taste buds is fat added to my body. However, Satan is quick to confirm what I already convinced myself: you shall surely not get fat! If we could only foresee the consequences of our actions, it would deter us from doing many things.

The manager of a historical mansion in Florida was having a problem with tourists touching the bedspreads and curtains in one of the master bedrooms. The "Do Not Touch" sign seemed to encourage the visitors to touch them anyway. He decided to change the sign to "Wash Hands Immediately after Touching."

You can guess what happened. It immediately ended the touching. People thought the curtains and bedspreads were treated with a harmful preserving chemical.[1] They stopped touching because they envisioned unpleasant consequences if they yielded to the temptation.

The alcoholic never dreamed he would end up in the gutter when he took his first drink. But he could remember saying, *One drink never hurt anyone.*

The man who cheated on his wife never dreamed he would lose his wife and children because of yielding for one fleeting moment. But he could remember thinking, *Who will ever know?*

The fish that took the bait never dreamed a hook was inside and he would end up in the frying pan. He couldn't see the man holding the fishing pole at the other end of the line.

Eve never dreamed she would lose her innocence, bring down the entire human race, and be banished from the Garden of Eden as a result of taking one bite from a piece of fruit. It never occurred to her that Satan had been lying. His power lies in his ability to deceive people into believing they can get away with yielding to temptation without suffering any consequences.

Lesson 5: *The pull of the temptation increases the closer you get to the forbidden fruit.*

Many people want to play with temptation as long as they can, thinking they can walk away from it at any time. But it's not that easy, because the closer you get to the temptation, the more pull it has.

Adam and Eve had walked to the middle of the garden, and now they were standing under the tree looking at the fruit. The closer they got to the tree, the more likely they would eat the forbidden fruit. It is hard to pick fruit if you are a hundred yards away, but it's easy if you are at an arm's length.

Willpower grows weaker as you get nearer to the temptation. Just as Superman weakens as he gets near the Kryptonite, you will weaken when you get near the temptation. Martin Luther once said, "Don't sit near the fire if your head is made of butter." The closer you get to the fire, the hotter the fire feels to you. Even though the fire remains at the same temperature, the heat increases as you approach it.

A wealthy man advertised for a chauffeur to drive his car. After three drivers applied, the man gave a test to evaluate them. He asked, "How close to the edge of the cliff can you drive without going over?"

"One yard," the first applicant bragged.

The second driver boasted, "One foot."

The last answered, "I always try to keep as far away from the edge as possible."

The third applicant got the job.

The closer you get to the temptation, the more likely you will go over the cliff. The further away you are, the less likely you'll fall for it.

Once I've entered into temptation, the carton of vanilla bean ice cream has the power to get me off the couch and into my car, drive me down the road, carry me into the store, and walk me down the aisle to the frozen foods department. Once I am there, temptation's power is much greater than when I was in my home.

My temptation began with my thought to go to the store. That's also the easiest place to stop the pull of temptation. Cutting off the temptation by killing the thought at the beginning is the key to breaking free from temptation's pull.

Lesson 6: *You must run away from the temptation instead of trying to resist it.*

Adam and Eve had gone to the wrong place and were considering eating the forbidden fruit, but they still had not sinned. Most people in this situation would attempt to resist the temptation by trying not to do it. The Bible, however, never instructs us to "try not to do it."

When we try not to do something, we are like the country boy who was lying under a farmer's apple tree looking up at the apples. The farmer saw him from a distance and said, "Hey, you! What are you trying to do, son—steal my apples?"

The boy yelled back, "No sir, I'm trying not to!"

Most of us are trying not to. The harder we try not to, the more we fail. When we "try not to," we're attempting to resist the temptation using the power of the flesh. This is absolutely the wrong thing to do, because our flesh actually wants to yield. The very thing that got us into the temptation is now trying to get us out of it!

Trying to resist temptation in the flesh is like trying to

. . . fight off a lion with a leg of lamb.

. . . push a magnet away with an iron pipe.

. . . scare off a thundercloud with a lightning rod.

. . . put out a fire with a piece of dried kindling wood.

The flesh is the wrong weapon to use in fighting temptation. "The spirit is willing, but the *flesh is weak*" (Matthew 26:41). The flesh makes an attempt to resist, but its resistance isn't strong enough to overcome temptation's pull. Oscar Wilde once said, "I can resist everything but temptation." So can you! That's why we need to find a different battle plan than "trying not to do it."

It may surprise you to find that the Bible never tells us to resist temptation. God tells us to resist the tempter (Satan), but to run from the temptation. We are to flee immorality (1 Corinthians 6:18). We must flee idolatry (1 Corinthians 10:14). Are we to resist youthful lusts? No. We are to flee from them (2 Timothy 2:22). That's quite the opposite of standing there, trying to resist. If you try to resist, you will lose.

Of course, don't say yes to temptation. But don't say no to it either. Any time you get into a conversation with temptation, it will talk you into doing it. Rather than "just say no" in your attempt to resist, "just run away" from it.

A couple of boys tried to walk through a corral when a bull saw them and charged. One of the boys said, "Let's stop and pray."

The other boy said, "No, let's run and pray!"

They didn't need to resist the bull inside of the corral. They needed to run out of the area where they were vulnerable. That's what you need to do when you are being tempted. You must flee *out of the area of temptation*. You must exit the area you have entered into.

The only way I can break the pull of vanilla bean once I am in the frozen foods department is to get out of the store as quickly as possible. Temptation's power can be broken only by running outside the area of temptation.

God promises that when you are under the influence of temptation, He will make a way for you to escape it. You've "entered into" temptation, and now you need to "exit out" of it. Look for the exit door and run to it. Here is your escape clause: "No temptation has overtaken you but such is common to man; and God is faithful, who will not allow you to be tempted beyond what you are able, but with the temptation will provide *the way of escape* also, that you may be able to endure it" (1 Corinthians 10:13).

Joseph found the way of escape when he was being seduced by Potiphar's wife. He didn't stand there, trying to push her away. He fled from her presence and ran out the exit door (Genesis 39:12). Adam and Eve didn't need to stand by the tree trying to figure out the best way to resist. They needed to run away from the middle of the garden.

Lesson 7: *Forbidden fruit leaves a bitter aftertaste.*

Eve picked the fruit from the tree and thought, *Hey, I touched it and nothing happened. I thought I was supposed to die.* Actually God never said she would die if she touched it. He had given the command to not eat from the tree to Adam before Eve was created (Genesis 2:17–18). Adam passed the instructions to Eve, and something got messed up in the communication. Adam probably told her, "Woman, (her name wasn't Eve until Genesis 3:20), God said don't eat from the tree or we will die. Just to be on the safe side, don't even touch it, okay?"

But Eve did touch it. She decided to pick the wrong fruit, which was the last step before sinning. She was like the little boy who opened the cookie jar in the kitchen. His mother was in the next room and heard the lid rattle. She called out, "Johnny, is your hand in the cookie jar?"

He yelled back, "Yes, Mommy, but I'm not eating any."

That's where Eve was. Her hand was in the cookie jar.

Satan whispered in Eve's ear, "Come on, Eve. If you eat it, you'll become wise. I'm not asking you to eat the whole tree. I'm not even asking you to eat the whole piece of fruit. Just take one little bite, and if you don't like it—hey, the whole deal is off."

Eve thought, *Well, I guess one little nibble never hurt anyone.* She bit into the fruit and then gave it to Adam. After he ate, their eyes were opened, and they were ashamed of what they had done. Shame always follows sin. Hindsight is always 20/20.

It was the first and the last bite of the fruit they ever enjoyed. Forbidden fruit leaves the bitter aftertaste of heartache and regrets. The most delicious bite of the forbidden fruit is the first one, and we think the pleasure will continue with the second bite. But the second isn't quite as good as the first, so we take a third bite, trying to recapture the original thrill. Each bite gets progressively less satisfying, but the compulsion to eat increases until we must have the fruit *even though we don't enjoy it anymore*. At this point, we are now addicted to forbidden fruit.

Lesson 8: *If you will eat the fruit that God has provided, you won't be hungry for forbidden fruit.*

God had given Adam and Eve all the trees of the garden to eat from—except one. If they had been eating from the fruit God had provided for them, they would not have been hungry for the forbidden fruit.

When God created Adam, he gave him a hunger drive, which is a need to eat. Then he provided fruit trees, a legitimate source of food, to satisfy his hunger drive. Temptation is trying to fulfill a legitimate God-given drive in an illegitimate way. When Adam and Eve became hungry for forbidden fruit, they were attempting to satisfy their hunger drive in an illegitimate way.

It's never a good idea to inspect forbidden fruit, especially on an empty stomach. Fulfilling their hunger drive with the right fruit would have kept them from being hungry for the wrong fruit.

Suppose you go to your grandmother's house for Thanksgiving, and she has just baked your favorite dessert, homemade apple pie. You are about to cut yourself a piece, when Grandma says, "You can't have that now. We're about to eat, and you can have it for dessert."

After eating a couple of helpings of turkey and dressing, you push yourself away from the table. You're so full that you have to loosen your belt. Then Grandma brings you a large piece of apple pie and places it in front of you.

You groan and say, "Please take it away. I don't want it. I'm full."

Just a short while ago you were craving the pie, and now it's repulsive to think about. What happened? Your hunger drive has been fulfilled, so the temptation is no longer there.

What works with your hunger drives also applies to your sex drive and every other need in your life. If you will fulfill these drives in the right way, you won't look for the wrong ways to meet these needs.

Temptations begin when we quit eating fruit from the trees God has provided; this creates a hunger that needs to be fulfilled. If we fulfill our desires and drives by eating God's fruit, we won't be hungry for forbidden fruit. But the reverse is also true. If we have been stuffing ourselves with forbidden fruit, we won't be hungry for God's fruit.

The Key to Victory over Temptation

Galatians 5:16 says that if we will walk in the Spirit, we will not fulfill the desire of the flesh. God isn't interested in putting our flesh in a straitjacket, trying to restrain our evil impulses. We need a power greater than ourselves to displace our selfish desires. The only thing that will displace the desires of flesh is a genuine work of the Holy Spirit inside our hearts.

I once knew a man who was heavily involved with drugs. When he hit bottom and had nowhere else to turn, he surrendered his life to Jesus Christ. Immediately he knew God had forgiven him and given him a new start in life.

Not long after his conversion, one of his former acquaintances offered him some drugs. When he looked at the drugs in the other man's hand, what he used to crave was now revolting to him. "I had about as much desire for those drugs," he told me, "as if he had offered me manure!"

What happened to him? God changed the desires in his heart. When you yield to the Spirit's control, the Lord puts His desires within you to want what He wants. You'll start desiring what the Holy Spirit wants instead of the things that tempt you, and then He will fulfill your desires in His way. You can't walk in the Spirit and the flesh at the same time. It's one or the other.

When a mother visited her son at college, she was disappointed to see pictures of scantily clad women on his walls. She gave him a picture of Jesus and said, "Do you remember Him?"

On her next visit, she noticed all the risqué pictures were gone. She asked him what had made him change his mind. Her son explained, "When I put up the picture of Jesus, the other pictures had to come down."

Perhaps you keep losing your battle with temptation. Change your strategy. God promises to give you power over it (see Romans 6:14). Don't say no to temptation, but say yes to Jesus. Through the power of the Holy Spirit, you can and will walk in victory.

Chapter 6

UNFORGIVENESS

Who Is in Your Dungeon?

"For this reason the kingdom of heaven may be compared to a certain king who wished to settle accounts with his slaves. When he had begun to settle them, one who owed him ten thousand talents was brought to him. But since he did not have the means to repay, his lord commanded him to be sold, along with his wife and children and all that he had, and repayment to be made. So the slave fell to the ground and prostrated himself before him, saying, 'Have patience with me, and I will repay you everything.' And the lord of that slave felt compassion and released him and forgave him the debt. But that slave went out and found one of his fellow slaves who owed him a hundred denarii; and he seized him and began to choke him, saying, 'Pay back what you owe.' So his fellow slave fell to the ground and began to plead with him, saying, 'Have patience with me and I will repay you.' But he was unwilling and went and threw him in prison until he should pay back what was owed." (Matthew 18:23–30)

During the Revolutionary War, a pastor named John Miller learned one of his enemies was to be hanged for his crimes. Upon hearing this, Miller set out on foot, walking sixty miles to visit General George Washington so he could intercede for the man's life. The general, when he heard the request, stated he was sorry, but he could not pardon Miller's friend.

Miller said, "He's not my friend. That man is my worst enemy."

Washington replied, "Well, that puts matters in a whole new light." Seeing the preacher's forgiveness for his enemy, the general signed the pardon.

Miller quickly carried the document another fifteen miles to the execution site, arriving just as the condemned man was trudging toward the scaffold. Miller's enemy was set free that day—by the pastor whom he had hated and persecuted.[1]

In Matthew 18 we find a man who was the opposite of John Miller. Instead of setting his enemy free, he threw him into prison. We are all in the process of either locking people up in prison or setting them free.

The slave in this parable owed a debt of ten thousand talents. A talent was not a coin, as many people think. It was a measuring weight of eighty to ninety-five pounds. A talent could be a sack of ninety-five pounds of gold and silver coins. You can imagine how much that would be worth. Well, just think about ten thousand of those sacks of coins. That was how much this slave owed the king.

In today's currency, that would be about $50 million. Someone calculated that at a slave's pay, it would take about forty-five hundred lifetimes to repay the debt. Since he could not pay it off, the king decided to sell him on the slave market, along with his wife and children, and all that they had. Each family member would be taken to a different location, probably owned by different masters, and they would never see each other again.

So the slave became desperate and did something ridiculous. He made one last-ditch effort to keep this from happening. He threw himself on the floor before the king and wept uncontrollably. He could hardly get the words out of his mouth, but in brokenness before the king, he said, "Have patience with me, and I will repay you everything."

What a ridiculous request! It would take him forty-five hundred lifetimes to repay that debt. No king would be so foolish as to think he could actually do it. But when he looked at the brokenness of the slave, something happened in the heart of the king. Instead of feeling anger toward the slave, he felt sorrow. The king's pity quickly turned into compassion because the slave's humility had touched his heart.

You've probably felt compassion before. Someone touches your heart and you are moved to help that person. This king was so moved with compassion that he released the slave of the entire fifty-million-dollar debt! His pity for the other man outweighed the amount he was owed.

This is what God has done for you when you come to know Him. You have a debt of sin that's impossible to repay. But when you humble yourself before Him and plead for mercy, He forgives you of all your sins. The entire debt is forgiven.

You would think that the slave would be so grateful that he would forgive all his debtors as well—that the forgiveness he received would be extended to those he needed to pardon. But this was not the case. Instead, the slave found a fellow slave who owed him a hundred denarii, which was about fifteen dollars. This was a significant amount for what a slave made in wages, but it was minuscule in light of the amount he had been forgiven.

The fellow slave threw himself on the floor, just as the slave himself had done before the king. He even said the same words that the slave had said to the king, "Have patience with me and I will repay you." It would seem that these words would jog his memory—that maybe he would remember the forgiveness he had received so mercifully from the king.

But instead of forgiving him the debt, he seized the fellow slave and started choking him. With his hands firmly grasped around the fellow slave's neck, he squeezed off his air supply. As the man fell to his knees, gasping for air, the slave screamed at him, "Pay back what you owe me—now! Pay me now, I said!" Since the fellow slave could not repay the debt, the slave threw him in the dungeon.

Perhaps you are choking some people right now. In your mind, your hands are around their necks, and you are screaming at them to repay the debts against you. When they can't, you throw them into prison—the dungeon of your soul.

How many people are locked up in your dungeon? Every person that you refuse to forgive is imprisoned inside of you.

There they are. You can see them now. They are hanging there, chained to the walls. Some have been imprisoned for only a few days. Others have been locked up for months. And some have been in your dungeon for years.

Every time you recall a hurtful memory, you make a trip down the stairs into the dark dungeon of your soul. You pull out your whip and lash the prisoners chained to the walls, making them pay for their crimes against you.

Your father is chained to that wall. He has been down there ever since you were a child. Out of your pocket you pull a list of the mistakes he made as a parent. After you read the list aloud to him, you yell, "You did all these things to me, and I'm going to make you pay!" You take your whip and flog him for each offense as he hangs helplessly in his chains.

Then you move on to the next person, a woman who talked about you behind your back. She was a vicious gossip who hurt you deeply, so now it's time for her to pay, and it's your turn to get even. You pull out your whip and beat her unmercifully until she is unconscious.

You go from prisoner to prisoner until every unforgiven person has been brutally punished. You turn to look around the room to make sure you haven't missed anyone. Everyone has been accounted for, so you put your whip under your arm and walk back up the stairs. This is your secret world, the dungeon of your soul. No one outside your dungeon knows what you do down there.

Although you should feel relieved after serving justice to these people, you don't. Instead, you feel a sharp pain inside your stomach. It is almost as if, instead of whipping them, you were whipping yourself on the inside.

You realize that you have no real satisfaction in tormenting those people. The constant thinking about them and what they did to you is wearing you out. You can't sleep. You toss and turn all night. Deep down in your heart, you know you must forgive and release those prisoners from your dungeon, but you don't know how.

Before you can be set free, you must ask yourself, *Am I willing to let go of my past hurts? Am I willing to release those who have hurt me? Or do I want to keep them imprisoned a little longer?*

Keys to Unlocking the Chains

It takes all six of the following keys to unlock the chains and release the prisoners from your dungeon.

Key 1: *You must base your forgiveness on what God has done for you, rather than on what the person has done to you.*

You might think that what the person did to you is too big a debt to forgive. Nearly everyone uses that as an excuse. If you base your forgiveness on whether they deserve to be let off the hook, you'll never forgive anyone! Whatever they did is insignificant compared to the debt God has forgiven you. It's like the fifteen-dollar debt compared to the 50-million-dollar debt. The two don't even come close in comparison.

The first principle of forgiveness is this: I cannot give away something I haven't first received. I can't give you fifteen dollars unless I have first received fifteen dollars. I also can't give forgiveness to others unless I have first received forgiveness from God. If He has given me $50 million, then it will be easy for me to give away fifteen dollars. My forgiveness isn't based upon how much someone owes me, but upon the abounding mercy God has granted me through Christ's death on the cross.

Key 2: *You must let God heal your wounds from the past.*

Unforgiveness means you desire to hurt the people who have wounded you. It's like the little boy who was sitting on a park bench in obvious agony. A man walking by asked him what was wrong.

"I'm sitting on a bumble bee," the boy explained.

"Then why don't you get up?"

The boy replied, "Because I figure that I am hurting him more than he is hurting me."

The healing process begins when you get up off the park bench. God will heal your wounds only when you stop inflicting pain upon the one who hurt you. If you don't let God heal your wounds from the past, those hurts will turn into hate. The seed of unforgiveness will sprout into the root of bitterness (see Hebrews 12:15), and the hurt you submerge will become a land mine. Then when someone places the slightest pressure on your hurt, you explode. You must get up off the park bench and ask God to heal your wounds. And then you must let Him do it.

Key 3: *You must feel compassion for the person who hurt you.*

Whenever we refuse to forgive others, we love justice more than mercy. We want God to execute judgment on our enemies instead of extending His compassion. God tells us what He wants:

> And what does the LORD require of you?
> To act justly and to love mercy
> and to walk humbly with your God. (Micah 6:8 NIV)

Notice that God wants us to *act justly*, but He wants us to *love mercy*. Justice is good, but mercy is better. "For judgment will be merciless to one who has shown no mercy; mercy triumphs over judgment" (James 2:13). As long as we hold on to justice as the highest priority, we will never forgive.

God gave the prophet Jonah a message of judgment to preach to the people of Nineveh, "Forty days and Nineveh will be overthrown" (Jonah 3:4). If anyone deserved judgment, it was the Ninevites. They were extremely cruel. When they conquered in battle, they skinned people alive. They cut off their enemies' heads and piled them up in front of the city. They set women and children on fire, cut off people's hands, gouged out their eyes, and cut off their ears, noses, or tongues.

Jonah went up and down the streets of Nineveh, preaching his message of judgment. Amazingly the entire city repented! When they turned away from their evil ways, God relented from destroying them. This made Jonah furious. He thought their years of committing war crimes and atrocities shouldn't be dismissed so quickly. That would be like Hitler being forgiven for exterminating six million Jews, not to mention causing so many other deaths in his attempt to take over the world. Does a quick prayer of repentance make up for all the people who were maimed and killed?

Make no mistake about it. Jonah wanted the Ninevites to receive God's judgment, not mercy. After the city turned their hearts around, the Lord asked Jonah, "Should I not have compassion on Nineveh, the great city?" (Jonah 4:11). God wanted Jonah to feel compassion for them, too.

In the parable Jesus told, the king "felt compassion" for the slave. Forgiveness proceeds out of compassion, not anger. You might think that you can't forgive because you hurt too much, but the pain won't go away until you forgive. It's impossible to forgive if you still feel hate for the person, so you must change the way you view the offender. You must now look at your enemy with compassion.

Every time Jesus felt compassion for someone, he saw a real need inside the person. To have compassion for people, you must look through the eyes of Jesus at their real needs.

Suppose you see a puppy that's whimpering because its leg is hurt. You suddenly have an overwhelming feeling of pity for the dog. You pick it up, cuddling it, saying "Oh, you poor little thing. It's going to be okay." You're so moved with compassion that you'll do anything to help it.

Those same feelings that you would have for a wounded puppy you must have for your enemy. Your anger must change to genuine pity, so that you can see them in a different light. How is that possible? Only through yielding to the Holy Spirit.

Years ago a friend turned against me for no apparent reason and started slandering me. I called him to find out why he was doing it. "I think you must have misunderstood me for some reason," I said. "Can we get together to talk about this?"

"No!" he yelled and hung up the phone. It disturbed me that he had no interest in resolving whatever bothered him, and I couldn't do anything about it.

A couple of years later, my wife and I were shopping in a store when he came over to talk with us. At first I thought he was going to apologize for his wrongful gossip. Instead, he just asked about how we were doing, acting like he had done nothing wrong.

As he continued to talk, I looked down and occasionally glanced up at him. I said a few words but didn't engage him in conversation. When he walked away, my wife said, "Kent, you hardly even looked at him while he was talking."

Her comment made me realize that I hadn't completely gotten over what he had done. I thought I had forgiven him but apparently not. I looked at him as he walked away and prayed, "Lord, I choose to forgive him."

Instantly something happened inside my heart. I felt compassion for him! My heart went out to him in a way that's hard to describe. My hurt feelings were gone. Later I went to him and asked how his family was doing. He never apologized, but it didn't matter to me anymore.

Many people hurt other people because they themselves are hurting inside. Wounded people will hurt others by releasing their hostility on them. They have a need for their inner wounds to be healed. Sometimes people don't realize how much they are hurting others. As Jesus had His hands and feet nailed to the cross, He said, "Father, forgive them; for *they do not know* what they are doing" (Luke 23:34).

Did they know what they were doing? In one sense they did. They had crucified hundreds of criminals. But in the spiritual realm they were blind and didn't understand what they were doing. Many people who have hurt us are also completely blind to injury they have caused.

If they never apologize to you, you can rest assured that the Lord knows how to make things come out even. "Never take your own revenge, beloved, but leave room for the wrath of God, for it is written, 'Vengeance is Mine, I will repay,' says the Lord" (Romans 12:19). Since God says to "never take your own revenge," you don't need to settle the score. Trust the Lord to take care of it, however He so desires. Ultimate justice is in His hands, but He would prefer for them to repent so He could show them mercy instead of judgment.

Key 4: *You must choose to pay off the debt they owe you.*

The king forgave the slave of his debt. That didn't mean the debt disappeared. It meant the king decided to pay off the slave's debt rather than make the slave pay. It cost him something to forgive the slave, but somebody had to pay the debt. It could not be ignored.

The cost of forgiveness is always borne by the one who does the forgiving. If I break your expensive vase and you forgive me, you suffer the loss and I go free. If I ruin your reputation and you forgive me, you experience the hurt but I go free. The amount you forgive is the amount you lose. However, God promises that He will more than make it up to you by rewarding you in eternity for your kindness. Jesus said, "But love your enemies, and do good, and lend, *expecting nothing in return*; and *your reward will be great*" (Luke 6:35).

People owe different kinds of debts. Some owe the debt of money. Maybe someone has borrowed money and hasn't paid it back, just as in this parable. Some owe the debt of gratitude. We've done things for people, and they haven't thanked us for it, but they should. Some debts are apologies that people owe. They have done something wrong and owe us an apology, but they have yet to apologize. Now we understand what Jesus meant when He taught us to pray, "And forgive us our debts, as we forgive our debtors" (Matthew 6:12 KJV). He meant all debts.

To forgive people of these debts, we must quit expecting them to repay us. Instead, we choose to free them of their obligations, just as the king did. We take our hands off their necks. We stop choking them, trying to get them to repay. And we make a deliberate decision to swallow the debt ourselves and never again ask them to repay it.

If you will do that, God will more than make up the difference for you.

Key 5: *You must stop replaying the hurt in your mind.*

Whenever we are hurt by someone, we record the incident on the DVR (digital video recorder) in our minds. Every time we recall an injury, we hit the play button and watch the hurt happen again. The remembrance of the event instantly brings back the painful feelings we experienced. And every time we watch the rerun of the offense, we get wounded one more time! The person may have caused harm only once, but because we keep replaying it, we experience the hurt a hundred more times. Our own unforgiveness causes the pain to be multiplied much worse than the original wounding.

When we forgive, we choose to stop recalling the past. Forgetting doesn't mean that we lose our recollection of past events, but that we choose not to keep remembering them. Because we have forgiven them, we make a decision not to call up hurtful memories in our minds.

If you delete a document on your computer, you click the delete button. Immediately a sign appears on the screen, "Are you sure you want to delete this file?" It asks this question to see if you really meant it. You have to click yes to get rid of it.

Many people think that they've forgiven someone, but they keep talking about their hurt. God asks, "Are you sure you want to delete this file? If you do, it means you've got to stop talking about it!" You know that you've forgiven when you quit bringing up your wounded past and get on with your life.

Key 6: *You must release the person from your prison.*

The king forgave and released the slave from the debt. You must release the person who has offended you. Let him go! Let her go! Unforgiveness will keep you chained to the one you don't forgive. If you don't let go, you'll take the unforgiven person with you wherever you go.

When you go to bed at night, the unforgiven person is there to keep you awake. When you go on vacation, the unforgiven person travels with you to your destination. You can't get away from him. Wherever you look, he's there ruining the trip.

The only way to get unchained is to forgive and release the person who has offended you. Unless you unlock the chains and release him, you will remain chained to him until you go to your grave.

I once attended a Bible conference where the speaker was teaching this parable about the king forgiving the slave of the fifty-million-dollar debt. He pointed out that the king not only forgave the slave, but also released him. The speaker explained that he himself had been hurt by four different people, and he had unwittingly held grudges against them. The Holy Spirit convicted him of his own unforgiveness, which compelled him to forgive and release each one. He then told about four amazing miracles that took place with each person as a result of his forgiving them.

I can honestly tell you that I've never heard a more powerful sermon in my entire life. It convicted me so heavily that I went back to my motel room and cried deeply in repentance. I realized that I had two people in the dungeon of my soul whom I needed to release. One man had caused me a great deal of grief and heartache through some hateful things he had done.

The other man in my dungeon was a friend whom I had led to the Lord, but instead of coming to our church, he joined another church in town. That's a crazy reason to have someone in my dungeon, but I held a grudge against him for that.

I prayed in my motel room, "Lord, I forgive and release these two men from the dungeon of my soul." When I let them out, a gigantic weight was lifted off me that I hadn't realized I was carrying.

A few days later, I was at home when my doorbell rang. To my surprise, the first man who had done the hateful things was standing at the door, crying his eyes out. He begged me to forgive him. I told him that I had forgiven him, and he has been a good friend ever since that day.

About a week later, on a Sunday morning just before church began, I was shocked to see the second man walking into our church with his family. He said, "I was going to a different church, but the Lord showed me that I'm supposed to come here."

I believe something happens in the spiritual realm when we forgive and let people out of our dungeons. A few verses before the account of the parable of the unmerciful slave, Jesus said, "Whatever you bind on earth shall be bound in heaven; and whatever you loose on earth shall have been loosed in heaven" (Matthew 18:18). When I let those two men out of my dungeon, this released them in the spiritual realm and allowed God to convict them of their attitudes. But as long as we "bind" people with our unforgiveness, they will remain bound, and it will be difficult for them to change.

You need to make one more trip down into your dark dungeon. Walk down the stairs one more time. As you open the windows, light shines brightly inside. Your prisoners squint as they see you approach, expecting you to beat them again.

But this time it is different. Instead of pulling out your whip, you take out the key of forgiveness. You walk over to your father, the gossip, and everyone else in your dungeon, unlock their chains, and announce to them:

> "I'm letting you out now. I'm not going to whip you anymore. I'm setting you free. I release you from the prison that I have kept you in. But before you leave, I plead with you, will you forgive me for keeping you imprisoned for so long and torturing you for all these years?"

You watch them walk up the stairs and leave your dungeon. It is empty now. All that is left are the unlocked chains hanging on the walls. It's been years since the dungeon has been empty. You can't explain it, but that sharp pain in your stomach is gone. You're no longer being tormented inside. Peace and calmness flood your soul.

Now you see that it wasn't them whom you set free. It was you!

Chapter 7

Canceling Guilt Trips

But the chief priests and the elders persuaded the multitudes to ask for Barabbas and to put Jesus to death. But the governor said to them, "Which of the two do you want me to release for you?" And they said, "Barabbas." Pilate said to them, "Then what shall I do with Jesus who is called Christ?" They all said, "Crucify Him!" And he said, "Why, what evil has He done?" But they kept shouting all the more, saying, "Crucify Him!"

When Pilate saw that he was accomplishing nothing, but rather that a riot was starting, he took water and washed his hands in front of the crowd, saying, "I am innocent of this Man's blood; see to that yourselves." And all the people said, "His blood shall be on us and on our children!" (Matthew 27:20–25)

When Pilate turned Jesus over to the crowd to be crucified, he must have felt terribly guilty. He didn't want to do it. He couldn't find anything wrong with Jesus, but the desire to please the crowd was just too great. So he bowed down to pressure from the crowd, released the criminal, and sentenced the innocent man to be crucified. Then Pilate went over to a bowl of water, washed his hands in front of the multitude, and told them, "I am innocent of this Man's blood."

Innocent? If he really thought he was innocent, why did he wash his hands? People don't wash their hands unless they are dirty. Pilate's problem was he washed his hands rather than his heart. Hands don't sin. Hearts do. The washing of hands will never cleanse a guilty conscience.

Pilate, after delivering up Jesus to be crucified, was trying to find a method to remove his guilt. It didn't work. I am certain when he went to bed that night, he didn't get much sleep.

God has put a conscience within us that works like an alarm clock. Romans 2:15 tells us that our conscience bears witness with thoughts that either accuse us or defend us. Whenever we sin against God, the alarm goes off, alerting us to the fact that we've done something wrong even if we claim to be innocent.

In a San Diego courtroom two men were on trial for robbery. A witness to the crime was asked, "Were you at the scene when the robbery took place?"

The witness replied, "Yes."

"And did you observe the two robbers?"

Again, the witness answered, "Yes."

The prosecuting attorney turned up the intensity and with a booming voice asked, "And are those two men in the courtroom today?"

Before the witness could answer, the two defendants raised their hands![1] Although they claimed to be innocent, their consciences gave them away.

Pilate claimed innocence, but his conscience was eating away at him. He tried to get rid of his guilt by scrubbing his hands. And just like Pilate, we try to remove our guilt by using the wrong methods.

Wrong Methods of Guilt Removal

Method 1: *Blame It on Someone Else*

This is the method Pilate used. Pilate said to the crowd, "This isn't my fault. It's *your* fault." The Blame-It-on-Someone-Else Method simply shifts the blame off yourself onto someone else. To err is human. To blame it on someone else is also human.

One day when my son Scott was two years old, I heard him crying. I went into his room and my daughter Hannah, who was four, was there also. A plastic bat was lying on the floor.

"What happened to Scott?" I asked.

"He hit his head," Hannah answered.

"On what?"

She pointed toward the bat on the floor and said, "The bat."

"Where was the bat?"

She said, "In my hand."

We learn the Blame-It-on-Someone-Else Method at such an early age. This method is not new. It goes all the way back to the Garden of Eden. After Adam sinned against God, he felt guilty. He needed some advice, so he made an appointment with psychiatrist Sigmund Freud.

Adam said, "I feel so guilty. What should I do?"

Freud answered, "It's simple. Blame it on your mother."

"But I don't have a mother."

"Oh yes. That's true," Sigmund said. "Then . . . blame it on your wife. Where did you get her?"

"God gave her to me."

Freud pounded his desk and said, "Ah-hah! Now we're getting somewhere! You see, God is really the one to blame for this whole thing. If He hadn't given her to you, she wouldn't have given you the fruit, and you wouldn't feel guilty. Do you now understand that God is to blame for your guilt?"

God asked Adam, "Have you eaten from the tree of which I commanded you not to eat?"

Adam remembered Freud's advice and answered, "The woman that *You* gave me, she gave me the fruit and I ate it."

Then the Lord asked Eve what she had done. She got in on the blame game too.

"Don't blame me," she said. "The serpent made me do it."

Like a hot potato, Adam tossed it to Eve, who tossed it to the serpent. But God didn't ask the serpent because He knew he didn't have a leg to stand on. Neither do you when you try to shift the blame.

The Blame-It-on-Someone-Else Method: Blame it on God. Blame it on your wife. Blame it on your mother. But whatever you do, don't blame yourself.

When you blame others, you're attempting to transfer guilt from yourself to someone else. You'll never get rid of your guilt using this method.

Method 2: *Run and Hide*

This is the method Peter used. Jesus told Peter he would deny Him three times before the cock crowed twice. Peter told Him that he would never do anything like that. But he did. At the exact moment he denied Him a third time, a cock crowed. Immediately Peter ran away weeping and went into hiding. He used the Run-and-Hide Method to deal with his guilt.

We will respond in one of two ways when we sin. We can either run from God and hide, or we can run to God and receive cleansing. For the moment, Peter tried running from God. His shame was too great to face his Savior whom he denied.

Maybe you have felt this way, too. You believe you can't face God because of what you've done. So you run away from church. You run away from Christian fellowship and the support system that you need. You try to hide from God, as Peter did.

This is exactly where Satan wants you. As long as you are on the run, his work on you becomes easy. His job is to keep you away from God. If you're not a Christian, his goal is to keep you from a relationship with God. If you are a Christian, he wants to keep you from having fellowship with God. The Run-and-Hide Method is another ineffective way to respond to your guilt.

Method 3: *Deny and Cover Up*

This is the method Judas used. The person who uses this method pretends that nothing is wrong. Denial is refusing to admit there's a problem, which forces us to cover up what we've done. When Moses killed an Egyptian, he buried him in the sand to cover up his crime (see Exodus 2:12). By the next day, the murder had become known. Perhaps God had sent a windstorm and uncovered the corpse.

I heard about a woman who was pregnant and on a strict diet. She made her husband a coconut cream pie; after a couple of days, he'd eaten only half of it. One day she was cleaning the table and decided to sneak a bite. One bite led to another, and before long she had eaten the rest of the pie. She felt guilty about cheating on her diet and knew she either had to admit it or cover up what she had done.

There was only one thing she could do. She baked another coconut cream pie and ate half of it to make it look like the original pie. If we don't *own up* to the things we do, we are forced to try to *cover up*.

That's what Judas did. He had an amazing ability. He betrayed the Son of God and then sat down and ate with Him, acting as if everything was just fine. He betrayed Jesus for thirty pieces of silver and then went to the upper room for the Last Supper with Him.

As they were eating, Jesus said, "Truly I say to you that one of you will betray Me." Then all of the disciples asked, "Surely not I, Lord?" (Matthew 26:21–22).

Finally it was Judas's turn. He asked, "Surely it is not I, Rabbi?" (v. 25). Judas never could call Him "Lord." To Judas, Jesus was only a rabbi or teacher. With a sheepish look on his face, he asked, "Who, me?"

Judas thought if he acted innocently his guilt would go away. It didn't. His guilt eventually drove him to suicide. The Deny-and-Cover-Up Method doesn't work either.

Method 4: *Get Some Professional Help*

I am both amused and disturbed whenever I watch a talk show where people from the television audience are asked to call in to the program. Usually a panel of "experts" is featured to help people with their problems. The host is standing in the studio audience and says to the TV camera, "We have a caller from Dallas. Are you there?"

The caller responds, "Yes, I have a question. I've been carrying guilt for some things that I've done. I'm really depressed and don't know what to do. Can you help me?"

The host of the show says, "I'm sorry to hear that. Have you been feeling this way for a long time?"

"Yes, for several years now."

The host briefly discusses the problem with the "experts" who give their opinions. He tells the caller, "It sounds to me like you need to get some professional help. Thank you for calling." This is another way of saying, "We don't know how to help you!"

I want you to know that I am not against counseling. As a pastor I counsel people all the time. However, it's extremely important that you choose the right counselors to advise you. A diploma hanging on the wall doesn't necessarily mean the counselor is approved by God. "Blessed is the man who does not walk in the counsel of the wicked" (Psalm 1:1). An ungodly counselor will give you ungodly advice.

The problem is that some people think the answer is found in "getting counseling" rather than making changes in their hearts. That is why people keep going to counseling for years, even though they don't get any better. They assume that the counseling sessions have some kind of magical power to transform them. It doesn't work that way.

Suppose you go to a medical doctor and he examines you. His tests reveal you have a tumor, so he tells you to come back next week.

When you go to his office the next week, he says, "The tumor is slightly larger than it was last week. I don't want you to become alarmed, because this is to be expected. I will prescribe some medication to calm your nerves. Make an appointment with the receptionist to see me again next week."

The next week he takes more X-rays and tells you, "The tumor is slightly larger than it was last week. You will experience some slight discomfort, but I will prescribe pain medication to help you cope with it."

This goes on for several weeks. He diagnoses the problem, talks about the problem, and prescribes medication to help you cope with the problem, but he never solves the problem. He never operates to remove the tumor.

You would tell yourself, "Hey, wait a minute. I think this doctor is making his living off of my *not* getting well!"

One man who regularly visited a psychiatrist confessed, "I must be the only guy who ever spent $15,000 on a couch—and I still don't own it." Counseling, in itself, will never cure the guilt problem.

The Only Remedy for Guilt

The answer to the guilt problem is revealed by the crowd as they chanted for Jesus to be crucified. They said, "His blood shall be on us and on our children!" (Matthew 27:25).

There it is. That's the answer. The multitude gave Pilate the remedy to his guilt problem, and they didn't even realize it. The cause of Pilate's guilt was also the solution for his guilt. His guilt was caused because he ordered Christ to be crucified, and the blood Jesus shed at the crucifixion was the solution for it. But the remedy must be received for the guilt to be removed.

Guilt comes as a result of sinning. It's your refusal to let Jesus Christ pay for your sins. You have feelings of guilt because it's a natural consequence of sin. You're punishing yourself as you try to pay for your own sins, which you can't do.

However, when you let Jesus pay for them instead of you, you are cleansed from your sin and are declared "not guilty" by God. Your guilt is removed because it encounters something that's more powerful than itself—the blood of Jesus Christ.

> The blood of Jesus His Son cleanses us from all sin. . . . If we confess our sins, He is faithful and righteous to forgive us our sins and to cleanse us from all unrighteousness. (1 John 1:7, 9)

> How much more will the blood of Christ . . . cleanse your conscience from dead works to serve the living God? (Hebrews 9:14)

> Without shedding of blood there is no forgiveness. (Hebrews 9:22)

Canceling Your Guilt Trips

Let's not make this difficult, because it isn't. You can cancel your guilt trips in two easy steps.

Step 1: *Be honest with God and admit what you've done.*

No more covering up. No more pretending. It's time to 'fess up. David said,

> I acknowledged my sin to You,
> And my iniquity I did not hide;
> I said, "I will confess my transgressions to the LORD";
> And You forgave the guilt of my sin. (Psalm 32:5)

God loves it when you're totally honest with Him. He already knows what you've done, but He wants to see humility and sincerity in your heart.

A prince traveling through France visited the arsenal of Toulon where prisoners were kept. Because of his nobility, he was given permission by the commandant to release one of the condemned men. He went from cell to cell and inquired why they were there.

Each prisoner declared his innocence, saying he was falsely accused and did not deserve to be there. Finally he came to one man who said, "As much as I want to be free, I am guilty. I've committed many crimes and have nothing to say except that I deserve to be here."

The prince then yelled with a voice heard by all the prisoners, "You despicable wretch! What a pity you should be among so many 'honest' men. By your own confession you are bad enough to corrupt them all. You shall not stay with them another day."

Turning to the officer, he said, "This is the man. Release him at once."[2]

Whenever we justify ourselves, our sin remains. But when we humble ourselves and honestly confess our sins, it puts us in a position to receive God's forgiveness. Confession doesn't cleanse us from sin, but it opens the way to receive it. Only the blood of Jesus can cleanse someone from all sin. We don't need to confess our sins a thousand times. We need to confess them once and thank God a thousand times for forgiving them.

A woman called in to a Christian radio program and said, "I had an abortion seventeen years ago, and I've asked God to forgive me every day since then." She wanted to know if God would ever forgive her, and if she was going to hell for it.

The talk-show host said, "Suppose someone who did something wrong to you comes knocking at your door the next day to ask for forgiveness. You forgive the person, and everything is cleared up on your part.

"But the next day, the person shows up at your door and asks forgiveness again. You remind her that you already forgave her the day before.

"She leaves, but returns the next day, knocks on your door and again asks forgiveness. Again you remind her, 'I forgave you two days ago. Don't you remember? Don't you believe what I said?'

"This goes on day after day for seventeen years. Wouldn't you be frustrated because she didn't trust your word?"

The woman on the phone said, "I never thought about it that way before."

The host said, "When you asked Jesus to save you, He forgave you of all your sins. Confession means 'to say the same thing.' You need to say the same thing that God says about your sins—He died for every one of them."

When we confess our sins, we don't just admit that we've done them, but we agree with God that Jesus died for them all. Confession declares that the blood of Jesus is more powerful than sin. It doesn't matter how horrific the sin may have been; His blood can cleanse you completely from it.

Step 2: *Receive your cleansing by faith.*

The work has been done on the cross. The blood has been shed. The price has been paid. The only thing left is for you to receive His forgiveness. To receive means to take it for yourself. God offers it, but you must take it.

I could offer to give you a hundred dollar bill by holding it out with my hand. But until you reach out and take it from me, it will never be yours. The transfer must take place between giving and receiving. This is also true with God's forgiveness. Until you receive it, it's not yours.

When you reach out and receive His forgiveness, the blood of Jesus cleanses you from all sin. Once your sin is removed, your guilt leaves.

You don't need to feel guilty anymore because in God's eyes it's no longer there. You must come to the place where you trust what God says instead of the way you feel.

A Christian friend of mine was haunted for more than twenty years by something he did. As a teenager, he'd been driving his pickup truck with some friends riding in the back. They were flying down a gravel road, swerving back and forth when the vehicle hit a bump. The truck rolled over and a girl flew out of the truck bed. She was instantly killed.

My friend was devastated by this and felt responsible for what had happened. On Memorial Day every year for twenty years, he went the cemetery, put flowers on the girl's grave, and then would break down crying and begging God to forgive him.

Even after he accepted Jesus Christ into his life, he still felt tremendous guilt over the incident. Many times I told him that God had forgiven him and he needed to let go of his guilt.

He always replied, "I just can't forgive myself. I know God has forgiven me for everything else—but it's this one thing."

One day while he was praying, God opened his eyes to the truth that Jesus had died for all of his sins, not just some of them. He finally grasped the reality of God's forgiveness, and for the first time in two decades he let go of his feelings of guilt.

A couple of days later, he came walking into my office with his face glowing. He literally looked like a different person. With a smile on his face, he told me, "I'm finally free from guilt!" Then he said something that I'll never forget: "I'm so free that *it feels like it never happened*!"

That's how you know you're forgiven. God removes your guilt so that it feels like it never happened.

Once the Lord has cleansed us, we've got to change the way we view ourselves. We must not look at ourselves as unholy or unworthy but as completely clean in the sight of Jesus Christ. "What God has cleansed, no longer consider unholy" (Acts 10:15).

But what about the haunting thoughts of guilt that still come after you have received forgiveness? You must not forget about your spiritual enemy named Satan, who is a liar and an accuser. He has the ability to put condemning thoughts into your mind, and he will try to convince you that you're not forgiven.

Richard Hoefler's book *Will Daylight Come?* includes the story of a little boy visiting his grandparents when he was given his first slingshot. He practiced in the woods, but he could never hit his target.

As he returned to Grandma's backyard, he spied her pet duck. On an impulse, he took aim and let fly. The stone hit its target, and the duck fell over dead. The boy panicked. He took the duck and hid it in the woodpile, only to look up and see his sister watching him. Sally had seen it all, but she said nothing.

After lunch that day, Grandma said, "Sally, help me wash the dishes, please."

Sally told her, "Johnny told me he wanted to help in the kitchen today. Didn't you, Johnny?" Then she whispered to him, "Remember the duck."

So Johnny washed the dishes.

Later Grandpa asked if the children wanted to go fishing. Grandma said, "I'm sorry, but I need Sally to help make supper."

Sally smiled and said, "That's all taken care of. Johnny wants to do it." Again she whispered, "Remember the duck."

Johnny stayed home while Sally went fishing with Grandpa.

After several days of Johnny doing both his chores and Sally's, he couldn't stand it anymore. He decided to confess to Grandma that he had killed the duck.

"I know, Johnny," she said, giving him a hug. "I was standing at the window and saw the whole thing. Because I love you, I forgave you. I just wondered how long you would let Sally make a slave of you."[3]

The spirit of condemnation is when the voice of Satan comes to the child of God and whispers, "Remember the duck. Remember what you did in the past." He's trying to make a slave of you, even though God has already forgiven you.

God makes this promise to His children, "I will be merciful to their iniquities, / And I will remember their sins no more" (Hebrews 8:12). If God doesn't remember our sins anymore, then why should you or I keep thinking about them and feeling guilty? You have no right to remember what God has forgotten. If you need to be free from guilt, sincerely pray the following:

> Heavenly Father, I confess that I've (name the sin). Jesus, thank You for paying for my sins by shedding Your blood on the cross. I receive You into my life and the cleansing from all my sins. Since You have forgiven me, I will not feel guilty about it anymore, but I will thank You from now on for Your forgiveness.

If you have honestly confessed your sins and received God's forgiveness, you can be assured that God has forgiven you. Now forgive yourself.

Chapter 8

CHANGE

Breaking Out of Comfort Zones

And in the fourth watch of the night He came to them, walking on the sea. And when the disciples saw Him walking on the sea, they were frightened, and said, "It is a ghost!" And they cried out in fear. But immediately Jesus spoke to them, saying, "Take courage, it is I; do not be afraid." And Peter answered Him and said, "Lord, if it is You, command me to come to You on the water." And He said, "Come!" And Peter got out of the boat. (Matthew 14:25–29)

We're all surrounded by comfort zones—those invisible, psychological barriers that make us feel cozy and secure. Comfort zones develop around us after we have done things a particular way for a certain amount of time. They can make us feel so comfortable that we may never want to change the way we do things, even if we'll benefit from change.

It comes as no surprise that change is the greatest threat to a comfort zone. The only people who like change are babies with dirty diapers. Sometimes it's easier to keep doing the same things over and over again than to make adjustments in our lives.

Two construction workers had taken a lunch break and opened up their lunch boxes. One of them said, "Not baloney again! I can't believe it. I hate baloney. This is the third time this week I've had baloney. I can't stand baloney!"

The other one said, "Why don't you just ask your wife to make you something different?"

He replied, "I don't have a wife. I made these myself."

The fact is, most of the baloney in our lives we put there ourselves. If we ever want life to be any different from the same old baloney we keep serving ourselves, then we must break out of doing the routine.

Comfort zones aren't completely bad. They can build security within us. That's definitely better than insecurity. However, security is like money. It is a wonderful servant but a terrible master. Healthy security can be found in a loving home, but a different kind of security is found in a prison.

In a penitentiary the inmates don't have to make decisions. Food and shelter are provided. They never have to worry about making house payments or where the next meal is coming from. One reason some ex-prisoners commit crimes is so they can go back to the penitentiary where it's secure. The prison, which is designed to be punishment to them, becomes their comfort zone.

That's the danger for us also. We can become imprisoned by our own comfort zones. They can keep us from experiencing all that God has for us and can stunt our spiritual growth.

Imprisoned by Stage Fright

When a crab grows, it breaks out of its hard shell and begins the process of forming a new one. Its life span is marked by passing through successive shells. It continues to grow as long as it dares to break out of its shell. When it stops breaking through, the crab stops growing and eventually dies. The last shell becomes its coffin.

For me, life has been a continual process of breaking through shells. From grade school to beyond high school, I had a terrible case of stage fright. A person with stage fright doesn't want to be noticed. His or her worst nightmare is being the center of attention.

When I was in second grade, I needed to go to the restroom, but I was too embarrassed to ask the teacher for permission. Not wanting to call attention to myself or my problem, I refused to raise my hand and decided to "hold it." I couldn't hold it for long, so I wet my pants. After I had finished the job, the teacher asked each student to come up to her desk to show her our work. It was hard to cover up the obvious.

In fifth grade I faced another crisis. My part in the Christmas play was to walk across the stage. I didn't have to say any words, just walk. Sounds simple enough, but I sweated it for weeks. The ten seconds it took to walk in front of the audience seemed like an eternity.

In high school I avoided the stage at all costs. Then as a senior, as fate would have it, I was appointed to read the class poem at the senior banquet. As I held the paper, I could barely read the poem because my hands were shaking so much.

After graduating from high school, I thought all possibilities of being on stage were now behind me. But during my last year in college, God interrupted my plans for the future and called me to preach. What a cruel trick, calling someone with stage fright to do that job. Not only would I have to be on stage, I would also have to speak on it for long periods of time. Definitely outside my comfort zone!

My first few attempts at preaching were excruciating. Not just for me, but for everyone in the congregation as they watched me sweat, fidget, and stumble through the messages. Then, bless their hearts, they told me how wonderful it was. Thank God He forgives truth-stretching parishioners who show appreciation to beginning preachers. I hated public speaking so much that I would have preferred a torture chamber over preaching a sermon. I often thought, *Lord, is this really what You want me to do? Shouldn't I be doing something else?*

As you will discover in a moment, I eventually broke through this extremely tough shell. But along the way God had to teach me a few things. Here are five principles I've learned about breaking out of comfort zones.

Comfort Zone Principles

Principle 1: *When you break through a comfort zone, it will make you feel uncomfortable.*

God places many of His blessings outside your comfort zone and then asks you to come get them. If you ever want to receive things you've never had before, you've got to do things you've never done before. That means you will have to break through some comfort zones. Peter was about to break through one by stepping out of the boat and walking on the water.

The disciples were in a boat on the Sea of Galilee when Jesus came walking to them on the water. Any science student will tell you water won't hold up a person who tries to stand on it. But in this case, Jesus overruled the laws of nature and made the impossible possible.

Peter ignored what he had been taught in science class and thought, *I know it sounds crazy, but if Jesus can walk on the water, then I'd like to give it a try too.*

The comfort zone Peter had to break through was the rim of the boat. For him to walk on to the water, the first thing he had to do was step over the boat's side. He had to make a decision to leave the security of the boat for the insecurity of the water. Breaking through a comfort zone begins with a decision to let go of your security blanket in exchange for something that looks frightening.

Perhaps you need to do something you've never done before, but a security blanket is keeping you inside the boat. To break through your comfort zone, you must be willing to leave your boat and take a step over the rim. You will feel uncomfortable getting out of the boat, but this is normal and to be expected.

Principle 2: *To break through your comfort zone, you can't let fear stop you.*

A spy was once captured and sentenced to death by a general in the Persian army. Before an execution, the general went through an unusual ritual. He would give the criminal a choice between the firing squad or whatever was behind a big, black door.

Given the two choices, the spy deliberated before deciding to get it over quickly. After the execution by firing squad, the general turned to his aide and said, "They always prefer the known way to the unknown. People are most afraid of the unfamiliar."

"General, what's behind the big door?" the aide asked.

"Freedom," the general answered. "Behind the door is a passageway that leads outside, but only a few have been brave enough to open it."[1]

Fear is the big, black door that will keep you trapped inside your comfort zone. It's the strongest force keeping you inside the boat. To be free from your prison, you must be brave enough to open the door. Your desire to change must become greater than your resistance to change. Before Peter stepped over the rim, several terrifying thoughts must have run through his mind.

Fear of criticism asks, "What will the other guys think of me if I get out of the boat?" The biggest critics you'll have are those who stay inside the boat. They're the ones who won't take any risks. You can't let peer pressure control you. Don't let other people's opinions keep you from what you know you should do. You won't go wrong if you'll always follow God's lead.

Fear of failure asks, "What if this doesn't work?" Many people won't take the risk of breaking out of their comfort zones because they're afraid of failing. They don't want to be embarrassed in front of others if they aren't immediately successful. To keep safe and eliminate the possibility of failure, they'll stay inside the boat.

Failure is not falling down, but staying down. "For a righteous man falls seven times, and rises again" (Proverbs 24:16). The righteous person will fall down but will keep getting up. If you are bound by this fear, you'll never succeed because you won't attempt anything new or different. You've got to take some risks in life if you ever want to accomplish anything significant.

Babe Ruth set a record with 714 home runs in his baseball career, but few remember that he struck out 1,330 times on the way to that record. Jonas Salk discovered the polio vaccine, but not many realize he failed two hundred times before he found the right one. Michael Jordan is one of the greatest basketball players of all time, but he didn't make the basketball team his sophomore year in high school. He didn't quit playing because of one failure.

Henry Ford went bankrupt five times before he finally succeeded. Thomas Edison failed hundreds of times in his attempt to find the correct filament for the lightbulb. When an aide urged him to quit after several hundred failures, he replied, "Why quit now? We know of at least a hundred things that won't work." Learning from our failures is part of the process of being successful. None of these people could have accomplished what they did if they had listened to the fear of failure.

Fear of harm asks, "Am I going to get hurt if I do this?" Everything worth doing entails a bit of danger. A boy told his father, "Dad, I wouldn't mind being a hero, if I knew I wouldn't get hurt." Heroes take the risk of being harmed because their desire to rescue another person is greater than their own self-preservation. The blessing on the other side of your comfort zone will be worth taking that chance.

Fear of the unknown asks, "What is going to happen to me if I step out of the boat?" We want to know what we are getting into when we try something new. But that's not always possible. We might not have every question answered before we make a decision. Sometimes we must take a step into the unknown.

A mariner's chart of the east coast of North America and adjacent waters, drawn by an unknown cartographer in 1525 and now in the British Museum, has some interesting comments on it. The mapmaker wrote across the great areas of then unexplored land and sea the following inscriptions: "Here be giants"; "Here be fiery scorpions"; "Here be dragons." At some time in its career, the chart fell into the hands of scientist Sir John Franklin. He scratched out the fearful old markings and wrote across the map, "Here is God."[2]

You can imagine the fear the early explorers must have felt when they read that map. "I'm not going into that area. No way!" The fear of the imaginary dragons kept them from discovering new worlds. Only those who refused to obey their fears would dare to venture into those unfamiliar waters.

Peter could step out of the boat onto uncharted waters because he could say, "Here is God." He was not going to allow the imaginary dragons to keep him in the boat.

Principle 3: *To break through your comfort zone, you must take a step of faith.*

In baseball you can't get to second base until you take your foot off first base. Some people would like to grow longer legs so they could step directly from first to second in one huge step, without the risk of being tagged out. But that's not going to happen. It's going to take you several steps to get there, and it all begins by taking that first step of faith.

Peter and the other disciples huddled together in the *USS Comfort Zone*. A storm was rocking their boat when Jesus walked toward them on the water. Sometimes God has to rock the boat to get us out of our comfort zones.

At first the disciples thought they had seen a spirit. After all, isn't it easier to believe a spirit can walk on water than it is to believe a man can do it? But if any man could do it, it would have been Jesus. The way to find out was to simply ask Him.

Doubting Thomas no doubt would have said, "Lord, if it is You, make a bridge appear on the water between You and me." My suggestion would have been, "Lord, if it is You, stop this storm!" But impetuous Peter said, "Lord, if it is You, tell me to come."

Jesus answered, "Come."

Why did Peter ask Jesus to command him to come? Because to get out of the boat and break through his comfort zone, he had to hear a word from God. "So faith comes from hearing, and hearing by the word of Christ" (Romans 10:17). When Peter heard Jesus say, "Come," he received the word, and it produced faith. If we are going to break out of our comfort zones, we also need to hear from God, just as Peter did.

When Peter saw by faith that he actually could walk on water, he took a step of faith. He made a commitment with both of his feet to step over the rim. Unbelief keeps both feet inside the boat. Doubt takes one step out of the boat and keeps one foot in. But faith steps completely out of the boat. Peter totally committed himself to his decision by putting both feet out onto the water.

Faith in action will always shatter the stronghold of fear. To break through your comfort zone, you must take a step of faith through the fear barrier that keeps you inside the boat.

In the comedy movie *What about Bob?*, Bill Murray plays a man who is afraid of everything. He works up the courage to go to a psychiatrist, who tells him that the answer to his problem is to take baby steps.

Bill asks, "What are baby steps?"

The psychiatrist explains, "It means setting small reasonable goals for yourself, one tiny step at a time. For instance, when you leave this office, don't think about everything you have to do to get out of the building, just think about what you must do to get out of the room. And when you get to the hall, deal with the hall, and so on. Do you see?"

Bill Murray says, "Baby steps!" As he leaves, he takes six-inch steps as he's repeating to himself, "Baby steps . . . baby steps through the office . . . baby steps out the door . . ."

That first step of faith doesn't have to be a huge step. It can be a baby step—but just do it by faith.

Principle 4: *The reason you must break through is to fulfill God's will.*

Now this is important. When Jesus told him to come, Peter understood it was God's will for him to get out of the boat. You don't get out of the boat just to prove to people that you're brave. You get out in order to get into God's will.

After God called me to preach, I enrolled in Southwestern Baptist Theological Seminary. One Sunday night I was invited to preach at First Baptist Church, Olney, Texas. Shortly before church was to begin, I was as nervous as a mouse at a cat convention. Because of my stage fright, the mere thought of speaking in front of people was terrifying. I seriously considered telling the church that I wouldn't be able to speak because I wasn't feeling well. That would have been an understatement.

Finally I cried out to God in desperation, "Lord, why did You call me to preach? I hate this. I can't go the rest of my life feeling this way. If You want me to preach, You are going to have to change me, right now!"

At that moment I heard God clearly speak to my heart, "Quit thinking about what the congregation thinks of you, and start thinking about what they need to hear. I have a message for you to deliver."

Instantly I was miraculously set free from my stage fright! My shaking stopped. I felt God's peace calm my spirit. Suddenly I wasn't afraid to stand in front of the congregation because I had a purpose. When I heard God speak to me, it produced the faith to do His will. My desire to fulfill His purpose gave me the courage to break through my comfort zone. That night I stood before the people totally free from nervousness and shaking, and I boldly preached the message they needed to hear.

The same thing happened to Peter when he heard Jesus say, "Come." Peter was freed from his fears because he knew he was obeying the will of God. He understood it was better to walk on the water with Jesus than to remain in the boat. We won't make the changes we need until we understand that being in God's will is more fulfilling than staying inside our comfort zones.

Principle 5: *After you break through, it will be better on the other side.*

As Peter got out of the boat and started walking on the water, he was thinking, *One small step for man, but one giant leap through my comfort zone.* But after taking a couple of steps, Peter noticed the instability of the waves. His mind reverted back to his science class where he had learned the density of a man on top of water is greater than the density of water under his feet. A few quick calculations proved to be the downfall of his faith.

His faith converted into doubt, causing him to plunge underneath the water. He cried out to Jesus to save him. Not only had he forgotten how to walk on the water, he also forgot how to swim in it! Fear can paralyze us, not from just doing new things, but also from doing the familiar.

I'm sure a couple of disciples in the boat were quick to point out his inability to make it from point B to point J. "You just can't trust what Jesus says," Judas would say. Thomas would add, "I knew he wouldn't make it. Doesn't he know that it's impossible to walk on water?"

After Peter sank, Jesus said, "O you of little faith, why did you doubt?" If Peter had only little faith, then those in the boat had no faith. At least Peter got out of the boat.

Peter sank after he took his eyes off Jesus and looked at the storm. He didn't sink because Jesus deceived him or because it was impossible to walk on water. He went under because he focused on his circumstances rather than the Lord.

When we break through a comfort zone, we may sink if we take our eyes off Jesus. But remember, He didn't let Peter drown. Jesus stretched out His hand and lifted Peter up, and He will do the same for us.

Although Peter sank, he wasn't a failure. Those few steps made history. Twelve men have walked on the moon, but Peter walked on the water. That's something only Jesus has done.

Whenever we first break out of a comfort zone, we will feel uncomfortable at first. But not long after we make the change, we will experience a new freedom on the other side. Then we wonder why we didn't break through sooner.

You've probably been to a swimming pool where people in the water are having a great time. Someone yells, "Come on in. The water's fine."

You put your toe in the pool and then shrink back, thinking the water is too cold. But as you stand by yourself, you notice how much fun the people are having. So you decide to join them and dive into the pool.

At first the water shocks you because it's so cold, but after a few seconds you get used to it, and it begins to feel warm. You spend the rest of the day enjoying swimming, not even thinking about the few uncomfortable seconds when you first jumped in.

You broke through a comfort zone. It was uncomfortable at first, but you found enjoyment on the other side.

What comfort zones do you need to break through? God may be prompting you to do something that you've never done before. Perhaps you need to make a career change. Maybe you need to teach a Bible study, start a new ministry, or reach out to someone you don't know. Jesus is standing outside your comfort zone right now, calling for you to come. How will you respond?

Stop clinging to the rim of the boat. Put your feet over the side and start walking.

Chapter 9

WORRY

The Movies in Your Mind

"Peace I leave with you, My peace I give to you: not as the world gives do I give to you. Do not let your heart be troubled, neither let it be fearful." (John 14:27)

March 1994. Three men, mimicking a movie they had just seen, shot and killed a retail clerk and then robbed a store. Within hours the group struck again, robbing a florist and a pizzeria. Detective Doug Hummel, of the Oakland County Sheriff's Department, explained, "All of them had apparently watched the film (*Menace II Society*) several times and were acting out parts of it."[1]

March 1995. Fifteen-year-old Jason Lewis carried his father's shotgun into the living room of his family's mobile home, where he brutally murdered his unsuspecting parents. He had just seen the movie *Natural Born Killers* and was acting out what he had seen on the screen.[2]

June 1998. A woman on a cruise ship off Sweden climbed out on the bow and spread her arms, imitating Rose's famous scene in the movie *Titanic*. Her next action, however, did not go according to script. She lost her footing, fell into the ocean, and drowned. Nearly two dozen copycat incidences of people reenacting this movie scene on ships' bows caused the Passenger Vessel Association to issue a "Titanic alert" to its cruise operators.[3]

When was the last time you watched a movie? I don't mean in that cinema at the mall. I'm talking about the movies in your mind. Satan has produced a wide variety of films that he wants you to view.

A seat has been reserved for you. The popcorn is ready. The lights have been turned down, and the show is about to begin. Admission is free. All Satan requires is that you believe what you see.

He projects his films in the theater of your mind, trying to convince you that what you see is real. Worry makes every imaginary tragedy appear as though it's actually happening. The devil wants you to react to what you see, just as the people acted out what they saw in the movie theaters. By making deception appear as reality, he can manipulate your behavior.

Acting on Belief

In the days before cell phones, I knew a package delivery driver's wife in Kansas who received a phone call while her husband was on the road. A man in a professional-sounding voice said, "Mrs. Williamson, this is Dr. Chandler. I'm sorry to inform you that your husband is in the hospital with a life-threatening, unknown disease and may die. We need a hair sample from you immediately because we believe you may have also contracted this disease."

The terrible news jolted the poor woman. The man instructed her to get a pair of scissors and cut off all her hair at the roots so the hospital could run some lab tests. She obediently did as she was ordered, clipping off all her hair until she was bald.

After completing the caller's instructions, she asked what to do next.

The man replied, "The next thing you need to do is to wait for your husband to come home. I made up this entire story." The prankster then hung up.

Satan wants your perception to be based upon deception. This woman acted on what she believed to be true. She would not have cut off her hair if she had known it was a prank. She placed her faith in the voice of a stranger without any other verification.

We act, not necessarily upon truth, but on what we *believe* to be true. The devil also knows this, so he creates an unreal world through your imaginations. He will call you on the phone, claiming to be a doctor who cares about you. He tells you that you have a life-threatening disease, even without giving any proof. He knows if he can get you to believe his lies, you'll panic as though they were true.

He loves to project his disaster movies on the screen of your mind. As you watch these imaginary horror flicks, you'll experience agony and torment as you view every catastrophe imaginable.

Plane crashes. Car wrecks. Incurable diseases. Financial crises. Although none of the events have occurred, you writhe in anguish as you watch each terrifying scene. Your frantic imaginations manipulate your emotions like a puppet on a string.

A woman had pain in her hand, so she looked up arthritis in her medical book. After reading a couple of pages, she knew she had arthritis in every joint in her body. She read a few pages about ulcers. "Now I know what's causing the pain in my stomach," she muttered. As she continued to read, she realized she had nearly every disease in the book. She made an appointment to see the doctor.

After doing an examination, the doctor scribbled a prescription and handed it to her. The note read "stop reading medical books."

When you nurture fearful thoughts, you can convince yourself that the imaginations are real. Deception is fighting reality for control of your mind. Imaginations are decoys to trick you into fighting the wrong battles.

During World War II the Americans made hundreds of inflatable tanks and airplanes, the same size and shape as armored tanks and aircraft. Although the decoys wouldn't fool anyone up close, they looked authentic when viewed from a distance. The US Army used the phony tanks to trick the Nazis into believing American troops were entrenched in a certain location. The plan worked. The Germans attacked the dummy tanks and planes instead of the real ones.

When you watch horror movies in your mind, you'll torture yourself fighting the decoys. And you fail to notice the demon laughing behind the movie projector.

Slaying the Worry Giant

Worry torments so many people, but you don't have to be one of them. You can, and you must, slay this frightening giant. Here are five powerful tactics to use as you fight this battle in your mind.

Tactic 1: *Stop watching the movies in your mind.*

Stop the movie! You don't have to keep watching it. If a horror film begins to roll on the screen of your mind, take immediate action by deliberately casting down the imagination. "Casting down imaginations, and every high thing that exalteth itself against the knowledge of God, and bringing into captivity every thought to the obedience of Christ" (2 Corinthians 10:5 KJV).

You can turn off the film by commanding the thoughts to leave in Jesus' name. Not every idea that pops into your head comes from you. The devil will keep filling your mind with troublesome thoughts until you figure out that he's the source, and you are determined to close down his operation.

When the disciple Peter suggested that Jesus not go to the cross, He responded, "Get behind Me, Satan!" (Matthew 16:23). Although Peter had said the words, the thought had come from the devil. Jesus shut off the idea by commanding His spiritual enemy to go away.

The Lord has given His children authority over all of Satan's power. "Behold, I have given you authority to tread upon serpents and scorpions, and over all the power of the enemy, and nothing will injure you. Nevertheless do not rejoice in this, that the spirits are subject to you, but rejoice that your names are recorded in heaven" (Luke 10:19–20).

Satan must leave when you take a stand to oppose him. "Submit therefore to God. Resist the devil and he will flee from you" (James 4:7). If you will stand against the devil, he will vacate the premises and take his movie projector with him.

I'm not saying that the devil is to blame for every time you worry. Most of the time, you have chosen on your own to think those frightening thoughts. At other times, your spiritual enemy has planted them. In either case, taking authority over fearful imaginations is crucial to making those worrisome thoughts leave. If you don't forcefully take a stand, the movies in your mind will continue to torment you.

Tactic 2: *Replace worrying with praying.*

A husband asked his wife why she was always worrying. "You know it doesn't do any good," he said. "Yes, it does," she replied. "Over 90 percent of the things I worry about never happen."

Most of the things you worry about will never occur. The other problems that have you worried either won't be as bad as you think, or God will give you the grace to get through them.

Instead of worrying, release your concerns to the Lord in prayer. God designed prayer to be a courier service to deliver your problems into His hands. "Don't worry about anything; instead, pray about everything; tell God your needs and don't forget to thank him for his answers" (Philippians 4:6 TLB).

How do you transfer your problems to God? The same way you throw a ball to someone; you have to let go of it. You cast the ball to someone else, who catches it. You must release your problem and cast it into God's hands. I will talk more about casting your problems to the Lord in the chapter on burdens. If you still worry after you've finished praying, you never actually let go of it. It was just a religious ritual.

Worrying can be more stressful than actually going through what you fear. My son Scott transferred from a small private school to a large middle school in seventh grade. He had to make numerous adjustments and hated every one of them. He constantly complained about having to attend the new school.

I prayed with him every night and gave him some fatherly advice. "Scott, don't worry about it. It's not as bad as you think."

He responded, "Dad, it's not that easy. It's hard not to worry."

By November I noticed he hadn't said anything about dreading the new school. "Scott," I asked, "you seem more relaxed than you were a month ago. Are you still having problems adjusting to school?"

He answered, "Yes, but I quit worrying about it. I found out that worrying was harder on me than actually going through it."

Many people never learn that it's usually more draining to worry than it is to experience the thing they dread. Prayer can remove the weight of worry.

Tactic 3: *Trust God to take care of you.*

Worry never trusts. Trust never worries. You can't trust God and worry at the same time. If you're worried, you might as well be honest about it. Just go ahead and tell God, "Lord, I absolutely refuse to trust You with my predicament. I honestly believe that You won't answer my prayer or take care of me."

You're probably replying, "I would never say that!" Maybe not, but that's exactly what you're telling God when you worry. Placing your trust in God is the only permanent cure for worry. Trust always puts confidence in someone else. If you don't have confidence in that person, you can't trust him.

When you board an airplane, you're placing your trust in the pilot to control the airplane. That means you're not going to break into the cockpit and grab the controls, trying to fly the plane on your own. Rather, you keep your hands off the controls and place your life in the hands of the pilot. Depending on your amount of trust in the pilot, you'll relax and enjoy the flight, or you'll be nervous until the plane lands.

To trust God you must place your life completely in his hands. That means you'll stop trying to control every circumstance and you'll relax, knowing that your situation is in the Lord's hands. How do you know if you're trusting God? It's simple, really. Are you relaxed and at peace or worried and stressed out?

King Solomon said, "Trust in the LORD with all your heart And do not lean on your own understanding" (Proverbs 3:5). Leaning on your own understanding means you're trying to cure your worries with your logic.

Your logic will throw you facts, figures, and reasons, explaining that everything is out of control and there's no hope for you. Your mind will show you graphs and statistics, proving failure is certain and God couldn't care less about you.

When Jesus was dying on the cross, He "kept entrusting Himself to Him who judges righteously" (1 Peter 2:23). He threw out the statistics that said the odds of Him rising from the dead were impossible, and He simply trusted His Father. When we place our trust in God, we don't need an explanation about how the problem will get solved. We let the Lord worry about that.

Jesus once preached a sermon to a group of people who were being tortured by worry. He assured them, "So do not worry, saying, 'What shall we eat?' or 'What shall we drink?' or 'What shall we wear?' For the pagans run after all these things, and your heavenly Father knows that you need them" (Matthew 6:31–34 NIV).

In those days, people didn't know where their next meal was coming from. They didn't have canned food, refrigerators, and fully stocked grocery stores as we have today. They didn't have closets filled with clothes. They may have owned only a couple of garments. To get an idea of their poverty, this Old Testament commandment was given: "If you ever take your neighbor's cloak as a pledge, you are to return it to him before the sun sets, for that is his only covering; it is his cloak for his body. What else shall he sleep in?" (Exodus 22:26–27).

Today we worry about other things. We might say, "How am I going to sell my house?" "Where am I going to find a job in this economy?" "How am I going to pay for my kid's college?" "Where am I going to find a wife?"

Jesus told his audience, "When you worry, you're acting just like the pagans who don't believe in God. So I'm tell you right now, listen carefully, your heavenly Father *knows you need these things*."

He didn't say, "Your heavenly Father doesn't care about your needs. Now get back to serving Him!" God knows we must have certain things to make it in life. To keep us from worrying, He made this conditional promise: "But seek first the kingdom of God and His righteousness, and all these things will be provided for you. Therefore don't worry about tomorrow, because tomorrow will worry about itself. Each day has enough trouble of its own" (Matthew 6:33–34 HCSB). If you will make the Lord your first priority, He will make sure that all of your needs will be met.

Tactic 4: *Discipline your mind to take one day at a time.*

We worry about bad things that might happen in the future, and that's why it's so important to learn to take one day at a time. Although it's wise to plan for the future, you can only live today. Concentrate on getting through *this* day. My wife and I will often say to each other, "Everything's good today!" It keeps us focused on enjoying the moment instead of fretting about tomorrow.

Life is a cinch by the inch, but it's hard by the yard. Anyone can handle the problems for just today. God will never give you more than you can handle for one day. But we get into trouble when we start thinking about all the possible challenges in the future. That's trying to live more than one day at a time.

Imagine that 365 toothpicks represent every day in a year. If you bundle all those toothpicks together, you won't be able to break it in half. If you tie thirty toothpicks together to represent one month, you still won't be able to break it in half. But if you unbundle the 365 toothpicks and deal with one at a time, you'll be able to easily break all the toothpicks.

That's the way God wants you to live—one day at a time. By God's grace, anyone can handle one day. If you'll do that, the giant of worry can't torture you anymore.

Tactic 5: *Relax and enjoy life's journey.*

Worry will sap the joy out of your life. That fact alone is a good enough reason to stop worrying. You're not enjoying life!

Your mission, should you decide to accept it, is to enjoy your life. God didn't put you on this planet to torment you with worry. He wants you to enjoy the journey. Jesus said, "These things I have spoken to you so that My joy may be in you, and that your joy may be made full" (John 15:11). One of the reasons Christ came to earth was to give us abundant life (John 10:10). That means He doesn't want us to waste our time worrying, but to enjoy life to its fullest.

One day I was driving my car on a rural highway in Kansas. I was between destinations, with nothing to do but watch flat land and telephone poles pass by. Then God spoke to my heart, "Enjoy the moment."

Enjoy the moment? What is there to enjoy?

I then realized that enjoying life is a choice I make. The Lord was telling me to draw joy from every moment and not just the exciting times.

Those three words changed the way I've looked at my circumstances ever since then. I was missing the moments that I should have been enjoying. I got the message.

Do you get the message? Have you *chosen* to enjoy your life? If not, stop what you're doing and make this crucial decision by praying, "Lord, forgive me for worrying instead of trusting You. From now own, I purpose in my heart to enjoy the life that You came to give me. Thank You for giving me Your joy and a purpose in life! Amen."

Chapter 10

SELF-IMAGE

I Love Me, I Love Me Not

"What is your servant, that you should regard a dead dog like me?" (2 Samuel 9:8)

I love me.

I love me not.

I love me.

I love me not.

To love self or not to love self. That is the question.

Jesus said, "You shall love your neighbor *as yourself*" (Matthew 22:39).

I love me.

He also said, "If anyone comes to Me, and does not hate his own father and mother and wife and children and brothers and sisters, yes, and even *his own life*, he cannot be My disciple" (Luke 14:26).

I love me not.

These two apparently contradicting verses, both spoken by Jesus, make me wonder, *Should I love me or love me not? If God loves me, shouldn't I love me?*

And here's a bonus question. If Jesus commanded me to love everyone, why does He now tell me to hate?

No, Jesus wasn't commanding us to despise mom and dad. The biblical word *hate* doesn't always mean to "cease loving." In this case it is used as an idiom of preference, where one person is preferred over another. When Jesus says you must hate your relatives and yourself, He means that you must favor Him above everyone else. Christ wants to lead you, rather than letting anyone else control your life.

However, some people wrongly believe they must hate themselves—the very souls Jesus created and died for. If that were true, you should *want* to go to hell, which would be the ultimate hatred of self. Obviously, that can't be right. You would be fulfilling Satan's will, not God's.

The devil desperately wants you to see yourself as a worthless creature with no reason to live. He wants you to take your eyes off Christ and place them on yourself. Then you'll become focused inwardly instead of upwardly. Inferiority blinds you from seeing yourself as God's unique creation with a wonderful purpose to fulfill.

Author Leanne Payne has said, "If we are busy hating the soul that God loves and is in the process of straightening out, we cannot help others. Our minds will be riveted on ourselves—not on Christ who is our wholeness."[1]

The Comparison Trap

A man told his psychiatrist, "Doc, I think I have an inferiority complex. Please help me." The doctor ran a series of elaborate tests, then called his patient back into his office to discuss the results.

"Please have a seat," the doctor said. "I have good news and bad news. The good news is you don't have an inferiority complex."

"That's great," the relieved man said. "What's the bad news?"

"The bad news is you really are inferior."

Many people try to attain self-worth by comparing themselves with others. They think feeling superior will increase their self-esteem. However, comparison usually makes most people feel inferior. Paul warned about the dangers of using others as a measuring stick when he wrote:

For we are not bold to class or compare ourselves with some of those who commend themselves; but when they measure themselves by themselves, and compare themselves with themselves, they are without understanding (2 Corinthians 10:12).

When Moses sent the twelve men to spy the land of Canaan, ten spies compared themselves with the people living there and immediately felt inferior. They said, "All the people whom we saw in it are men of great size . . . and we became like grasshoppers *in our own sight*, and so we were in their sight" (Numbers 13:32–33).

The way you see yourself determines how you believe others view you. The ten spies saw themselves as grasshoppers ("in our own sight") and believed their enemies also saw them that way ("so we were in their sight"). If you see yourself as inferior, then you believe everyone else sees you as inferior. If you view yourself as a grasshopper, you will act like a grasshopper. I haven't seen any grasshoppers beating up giants lately. Have you?

Whenever you measure yourself with others, you wrongly interpret your self-worth. The comparison trap can be devastating. Someone is always bigger, stronger, faster, prettier. Just when you think you are winning the rat race, you run into faster rats. It's a frustrating way to live.

Mirror, Mirror, on the Wall

When you look into the mirror, you see the most unlovable creature gawking back at you. An inferiority complex draws your attention to four areas of introspection that produce self-hatred.

Physical appearance

Self-image is the way you view yourself. It's the self-portrait that hangs in the gallery of your mind. Some people have considered committing suicide because they hate the way they look. This is not the kind of "hating self" that Christ meant.

A popular attraction at carnivals is the crazy house of mirrors. Inside this maze of warped mirrors, you can view your contorted reflections.

Your eyes and ears balloon out of proportion. You see yourself as exceedingly skinny or overweight. You don't actually look like that, but the warped mirrors make it appear that way.

A distorted self-image is no closer to reality than the image reflected by the contorted carnival mirrors. When you look into the mirror, you're disgusted with your appearance. You focus on your unsightly features and exaggerate each flaw. My, what big ears, nose, and eyes you have! This dissatisfaction with your appearance can produce hatred toward the God who created you.

A Louis Harris poll showed that 56 percent of men would like to lose weight; 36 percent want more hair; 34 percent would change their height; 27 percent would hide signs of aging; and 19 percent would like a different nose. Women wanted to make even more changes. Seventy-eight percent of women weren't happy with their weight; 48 percent would hide signs of aging; 37 percent would change their teeth; 34 percent wanted different legs; and 18 percent would change their feet.[2]

Do you think having a nearly perfect physical appearance would help your self-esteem? A survey of twelve Hollywood actors and actresses proves it doesn't. They were asked, "If you could change something about your facial features, what would it be?" The answers ranged from four to twelve items per person. These people, admired by millions as the best looking in our society, weren't completely happy with their appearance.[3] It just goes to show that self-image isn't determined by the way we are, but what we think we are.

Intelligence

Don't let your IQ determine your self-worth. God makes his Albert Einsteins and his Forrest Gumps. He has also made sure that no one will ever know everything. Geniuses may excel in one field of expertise but can be ignorant in other areas. Will Rogers once said, "Everyone is ignorant, except on different things."

A person's intelligence doesn't necessarily guarantee success in the workplace. Karen Arnold, an associate professor of education at Boston College, and Terry Denny, a professor emeritus at the University of

Illinois at Urbana-Champaign, followed eighty-one valedictorians and salutatorians for ten years after their graduations. To the surprise of the researchers, most of these scholars achieved only average success in the workplace. Success can usually be attributed to attitude, diligence, and hard work, and not necessarily aptitude.[4]

Intelligence might even hinder you from receiving God's revelation. Sometimes your logical conclusions can keep you from trusting God to lead you in a different way (see Proverbs 3:5–6). Jesus prayed, "I praise You, Father, Lord of heaven and earth, that You have hidden these things from the wise and intelligent and have revealed them to infants" (Matthew 11:25). God has made truth so simple that a small child can understand it. God is more concerned with your "I will" than your IQ.

Abilities

The master in the parable of the talents (which were bags of coins) distributed five talents to one slave, two to another, and to another one, "each according to his own ability" (Matthew 25:15). God doesn't give everyone the same abilities. Some people may be extremely gifted in one area, while others are gifted in other ways.

God never gave abilities as a measuring stick to determine your self-worth. You've been granted certain capabilities so you can fulfill your destiny. The Lord has equipped you with certain skills to accomplish His will, and not so you can brag about your abilities. God wants you to use your gifts for His glory, not your own.

Success

Self-worth should never be measured by achievement either. Several years ago a successful businessman lost more than a million dollars in a bad investment. Someone asked him, "How much are you worth now?"

"I'm worth the same as I always was," the businessman replied. "I never calculate my self-worth according to my successes or failures."

While you should work diligently at your job, don't ever base your worth on your performance. What appears to be an insignificant job in your eyes can actually be of incredible importance to God. Jesus said that being a servant will make you great in God's kingdom (see Mark 10:43). Becoming a slave will elevate you to number one (see Mark 10:44). Even a cup of cold water given in Jesus' name will be rewarded in heaven (see Mark 9:41). Being faithful in little on earth will result in being in charge of much in eternity (see Luke 19:17). So what does this mean? Many of the things we do might not look that important from an earthly perspective, but they are significant assignments from God.

Other reasons for self-hatred

People hate themselves for other reasons: self-pity, feelings of failure, excessive introspection, guilt from past sins, rejection by parents or peers, and lacking purpose in life, just to name a few. God didn't create you so that you will find reasons to self-destruct. You will never function to your fullest potential as long as you view yourself as inferior.

Healthy Self-Image

Jesus said, "Love your neighbor as yourself" (Matthew 22:39). Why is this important? It's because you can't honestly tell someone that God loves him or her if you don't believe it about yourself.

A prison chaplain once told me, "Do you know why those prisoners committed their crimes? It's because they hate themselves. And if they hate themselves, how can they love others? If they don't have respect for themselves, why would they respect anyone else and their property? So it doesn't bother them to steal or kill. They don't love their neighbors because they don't love themselves."

This chaplain knew what he was talking about; he himself had been convicted of murder and sent to the penitentiary. While he was in prison, he gave his life to Christ. After he had served his time, he decided to become a chaplain. After all, who knows how a convict thinks better than an ex-con? He now spends his time teaching prisoners that God loves them and that they should love themselves as His creation.

Attaining a healthy self-image requires that you see yourself as God sees you. To have a permanent change in perspective, the Holy Spirit must reprogram your heart. Once God changes you within, you can view yourself in a spiritually healthy way.

How can you correct your warped perspective? Three steps are necessary.

Step 1: *Quit being selfish.*

Self can make one person feel superior and someone else feel inferior. Both attitudes are wrong, because everyone is equally valuable in God's sight. No one is greater or lesser in value than anyone else.

It's important to understand that *self* can mean a couple of things. It can mean "the person God created you to be," which is good, or it can mean "having a selfish attitude," which is bad. The Lord wants you to love yourself as His creation, but to hate your selfish attitudes.

When Jesus said to hate your own life, He meant to hate *selfishness*, not the person God created you to be. Selfishness demands its own way, sees itself as the center of the universe, and opposes the rule of God. Paul said, "I die daily" (1 Corinthians 15:31), which meant that he made a conscious effort every day to stop selfishness from telling him what to do. He also said, "I have been crucified with Christ; and it is no longer I who live, but Christ lives in me" (Galatians 2:20). Jesus will manifest His life through us when we die to selfishness.

Near the end of World War II, newspapers in Japan advertised for kamikaze pilots. They searched for volunteers to fly a plane on just one mission—to crash into American aircraft carriers. These suicide pilots were strapped in a plane with dynamite and given enough fuel to fly out to sea, but not enough to return. Once someone became a kamikaze pilot, he couldn't turn back. Before he departed for his mission, his family gave him a funeral. The pilot attended his own funeral, even though he was still alive.

Although you're still alive, you need to conduct a funeral for your selfishness every day. Jesus said, "If anyone wishes to come after Me, he must deny himself, and take up his cross daily, and follow Me" (Luke 9:23). You don't take up your cross daily to crucify Jesus again, but to crucify your selfishness. Each morning when you wake up, self wakes up with you and tries to rule your life. The cross is where self dies—and that's when you start living in resurrection power.

Step 2: *Accept yourself as God's creation.*

Some people have delusions of grandeur, while others have delusions of worthlessness. People who are disgusted with themselves direct their hatred toward God. They angrily shake their fists at Him complaining, "Why did You make me like this?"

God answers, "The thing molded will not say to the molder, 'Why did you make me like this,' will it?" (Romans 9:20).

The Lord wants you to accept yourself and love yourself as His creation. David said,

I will give thanks to You, for I am fearfully and wonderfully made;
Wonderful are Your works,
And *my soul knows it very well*. (Psalm 139:14)

David not only thanked God for creating him, but also realized that in doing so He had done a wonderful job.

You can acquire a healthy self-image by recognizing that God crafted you in your mother's womb and you are wonderfully made. It's not what you say about yourself that makes it true, but what God says about you.

Jesus said you are more valuable than:

- *Birds.* "Consider the ravens, for they neither sow nor reap; and they have no storeroom nor barn; and yet God feeds them; how much more valuable you are than the birds!" (Luke 12:24).

- *Many sparrows.* "So do not fear; you are more valuable than many sparrows" (Matthew 10:31).

- *Sheep.* "How much more valuable then is a man than a sheep!" (Matthew 12:12).

- *The entire world.* "For what will it profit a man, if he gains the whole world, and forfeits his soul? Or what will a man give in exchange for his soul?" (Matthew 16:26).

Christian psychologist James Michaelson once counseled a woman who felt lonely and abandoned. As she explained how she felt, he couldn't concentrate on what she was saying because a Scripture kept running through his mind: "It is He who has made us, and not we ourselves" (Psalm 100:3). This verse had no apparent connection with her problem, but he couldn't quit thinking about it.

After she finished talking, she sat in silence waiting for a response. Dr. Michaelson didn't know what to say other than quote the verse, although he realized it might sound foolish since it seemed unrelated to her dilemma.

"I think God wants you to know something," Dr. Michaelson said. "'It is God who has made us, and not we ourselves.' Does that mean anything to you?"

The woman immediately broke down, crying. After composing herself, she explained what it meant.

"I didn't tell you this, but my mother got pregnant with me before she was married. All my life I believed that I was a mistake—an unplanned accident—and that God didn't create me. When you quoted that verse, I pictured in my mind God forming me in my mother's womb. Now I know that God created me, and I'm not a mistake. I'll never be the same again! Thank you, Dr. Michaelson. I'll never forget this day as long as I live!"[5]

God knew this woman needed to know she was His marvelous creation and not an accident. Her perspective changed dramatically once she understood God had crafted her in the womb. Like King David, she discovered God as her Creator.

Can you say, "I am fearfully and wonderfully made"? Does your soul know it very well?

Step 3: *Stop viewing others as competition.*

Since a distorted self-image comes by comparing yourself with other people, you must stop viewing them as your competition. Instead, God wants you to look at them as valuable and worthy of your help. He says, "Do not merely look out for your own personal interests, but also for the interests of others" (Philippians 2:4).

First, by looking out for the interest of others, it gets your eyes off yourself, which is the main cause for your feelings of arrogance or inadequacy. Second, it fulfills the command of Jesus, "You shall love your neighbor as yourself" (Matthew 22:39). Both you and your neighbor are equally valuable in God's eyes. Your neighbor is not someone that you compete against, but someone to help in a time of need.

An incredible display of sportsmanship took place in a college women's softball game, when Western Oregon played Central Washington University in 2008. At stake was a bid to the NCAA's Division II playoffs.

"Never in my life had I seen anything like it," said Central Washington Coach Gary Frederick. "It was just unbelievable."

Central Washington was leading two to one when Western Oregon sent one of their worst hitters to the plate. Five-foot-two-inch Sara Tucholsky's batting average was an embarrassingly low .153. She had never hit a home run in her entire life, but this day would be different. Against all odds, Sara hit a pitch over the centerfield fence for an apparent three-run home run. All she had to do was run around the bases.

But when Sara got to first base, something went terribly wrong. She collapsed on the base path, having torn the anterior cruciate ligament (ACL) in her right knee. Writhing in pain, it would impossible for her to finish rounding the bases, which meant she would not be credited with the only home run in her lifetime.

"Our first-base coach was telling me, 'I can't touch you or you'll be out if I help you.'" The rules prohibited her teammates from helping her around the bases. If they touched her, she would be called out.

As Sara lay on the ground, the first baseman from the opposing team, Mallory Holtman, asked the umpire if the rules also disallowed the other team from carrying her around the bases. The umpire said that although her teammates couldn't assist her, nothing in the rule book prohibited the opposing team from helping her.

Holtman asked a teammate to lend her a hand. The two of them picked up Sara and resumed her home run walk, pausing at each base to allow her to touch the bag with her uninjured leg. By helping her complete her home run, they were also risking losing the ballgame, which would keep them from going to the playoffs.

"We started laughing when we touched second base," Holtman said. "I wondered what this must look like to other people. I looked up and saw the entire Western Oregon team in tears."

"My whole team was crying," Sara said. "Everybody in the stands was crying. My coach was crying." The Central Washington players ignored their goal of winning and going to the playoffs so they could help their injured opponent.

Western Oregon went on to win the game four to two. Because they assisted the other team, Central Washington never made it to the NCAA playoffs.[6]

Some things, like helping a hurting person, are more important than winning ball games.

When you swap places with others to feel how they hurt, you've taken the first step toward loving your neighbor as yourself. And you've also learned the secret to acquiring a godly self-image.

Now, where was I? Oh, yeah . . .

I love me not.

I love me.

Chapter 11

PESSIMISM

Treasure Hunting

"These things have I spoken unto you, that my joy might remain in you, and that your joy might be full." (John 15:11 KJV)

Roy Parrino has a job that most people probably wouldn't have on their career wish list. Can you guess what it might be?

Embalming bodies at the county morgue? Dead wrong.

Liposuction technician? Fat chance.

Roy works in a sewer in Orange County, California. He spends his days cleaning out miles of sewer lines in the Los Angeles area—braving toxic fumes, avoiding discarded syringes, and wading through filthy muck that's been flushed down toilets.

"You really have to psych your mind up for it," Parrino says. "Remember, you're going into the filthiest environment there is. It's like being in a big toilet."[1]

Maybe you feel like you're in a sewer right now. You're stuck in an unwanted job, surrounded by intolerable people. You're braving toxic attitudes, avoiding discarded relationships, and trying to fix unsolicited problems. It's easy to turn into a pessimist when you're surrounded by repugnant environments and repulsive people.

If your heart isn't in tune with God, you'll look for the worst in your situation. You'll overlook the good things you have and gripe about not having enough. When negativity consumes your heart, your perspective gradually deteriorates, plunging you into the sewer of pessimism.

Meet the princess of pessimism, Ima Whiner. She gripes. She complains. She looks for the negative in every situation. Even the Twenty-third Psalm isn't protected from her scrutiny.

A Pessimist's Commentary on Psalm 23
By Ima Whiner

The LORD is my shepherd, I shall not want.

"Shall not want"? Give me a break. I want lots of things. I'd like to have a nicer house, a better job, and a pay raise. I want people to do what I say, when I say. And I wouldn't mind winning the lottery either.

He makes me lie down in green pastures; He leads me beside quiet waters.

I have a problem with the words *makes me*. That sounds a bit bossy to me. First You say I can't want things; now You're making me do things.

He restores my soul; He guides me in the paths of righteousness for His name's sake.

I don't want to be guided down the paths of righteousness. I prefer the more scenic routes. How about leading me to Hawaii for a change? What about Vegas? I'm getting a little tired of the paths of righteousness. The next thing you know, You'll be leading me down a dark alley.

Even though I walk through the valley of the shadow of death, I fear no evil; for You are with me.

What am I doing walking through the valley of the shadow of death? I thought I was supposed to be lying down in green pastures. Did You take a wrong turn, or what? And You call Yourself a shepherd?

Your rod and Your staff, they comfort me.

> To tell You the truth, a rod and staff are not my idea of comfort. A rod and reel, I'll take. A back massage would be even better. Skip the rod and staff.

You prepare a table before me in the presence of my enemies.

> Great. Out of all the restaurants in the world, You choose the one where my enemies like to eat. I'm sure I'll relish every bite of that meal.

You have anointed my head with oil; My cup overflows.

> I don't want any oil on my head. I prefer shampoo. And for good-ness' sake, can't You stop pouring before my cup overflows? What kind of waiter are You anyway? How would You like to have hot coffee spilled all over Your hand?

Surely goodness and lovingkindness will follow me all the days of my life, And I will dwell in the house of the LORD forever.

> I don't want to be confined to a house forever. That sounds like a prison. It might be nice to step outside once every thousand years or so. I never will understand why so many people love the Twenty-third Psalm.

Do you view your circumstances like Ima Whiner?

What Are You Looking At?

Although you may not choose your circumstances, you do choose how you view them. To improve your outlook, you must go treasure hunt-ing. Every situation contains both good and bad, but you decide which you look for.

Your heart works like a video camera. The cameraman inside your heart points his camera to what you want to focus on. He can zoom in on an object or zoom out to get a bigger perspective. As you travel through life, the cameraman inside your heart is constantly zooming in on positive or negative objects.

Long ago a king called two servants before his throne. He told the first, "I want you to travel throughout my kingdom and bring back a sample of every weed you can find." He told the second, "I want you also to journey throughout my kingdom and bring back a sample of every flower you can find."

Six months later the first servant returned. The king asked, "Have you carried out my command?" The servant answered, "I have, and I am amazed to find so many weeds. In fact, there's nothing but weeds in your kingdom."

A few minutes later the second servant returned. The king asked him, "Have you carried out my command?" He answered, "I have, and I am amazed to find so many beautiful flowers. In fact, there's nothing but flowers in your kingdom."[2]

Jesus said, "Seek, and you will find" (Luke 11:9). Whatever you seek, you will find. Zoom in on weeds, you won't see flowers. Zoom in on flowers, you won't see weeds.

Moses sent the twelve spies into the land of Canaan, asking them to bring back a report. Ten zoomed in on weeds. Two saw flowers. Although all twelve men scoped out the same property, they focused on different things and gave opposite reports. Ten looked at the land flowing with milk and honey and saw only calories and cholesterol. Joshua and Caleb inspected the same piece of real estate and saw a future homeland.

Every day God asks you to report on the land where you live. In every situation you must decide whether you're going to look for weeds or flowers. Like those spies from thousands of years ago, most people today choose to make their lives miserable by looking for what's wrong.

"You Might Be a Pessimist If . . ."

Jeff Foxworthy is probably best known for his "you might be a redneck if" jokes. He gives a description of how a redneck acts and talks, so you can identify such a person. You can also identify a pessimist by how he or she acts and talks. **You might be a pessimist if . . .**

You expect the worst to happen.

A man decided to start a hot dog business. He bought a cart, filled it with hot dogs, and pushed it down a busy city street during the lunch hour. He sold out, so he ordered more from his supplier. As the weeks passed, he kept expanding his business and became a successful vendor.

One day his son came home from college and gave him some advice.

"Dad, don't you know what's going on in the business world? Things are bad. We are in a depression."

His father replied, "We are? I guess I'd better cut back on my supply of hot dogs."

So he did. He reduced his inventory, only ordering minimum quantities. Because he kept running out, his frustrated customers stopped buying from him. Several months later he shut down his business.

That night he called his son at college and said, "Son, you were right. We are in a depression!"

The way you choose to see the world creates the world you see. Pessimists expect the worst to happen, which often becomes a self-fulfilling prophecy. Negative attitudes can produce negative circumstances. A pessimistic outlook on life will create a depressing world to live in, just like the man's hot dog business.

You can't see the big picture.

Pessimism restricts your perspective and gives you tunnel vision, which blinds you to the big picture.

A motivational expert lectured a group of business professionals about depression. She took a large sheet of white paper, drew a small black dot in the middle, and posted it on a bulletin board in front of the class. She asked a man in the front row what he saw.

"A black spot," he responded.

A woman seated in the back raised her hand and said, "I would say it is more accurately called a little dot."

The lecturer asked if anyone else could describe what he or she saw. A man blurted out, "A speck."

She told the class, "You all saw the little black dot, but none of you noticed the big white sheet of paper. That's my speech. You can all go home now."

You will get depressed if you are so absorbed with the little details that you miss the big picture. A closed-in viewpoint narrows your perspective, leaving God outside your scope of vision. To get the proper perspective, the cameraman in your heart must zoom out, which brings God's blessings into view.

Pessimism always looks at a situation and leaves God out of the picture. Joseph in the Old Testament had a dream where he and his brothers were binding sheaves in the field. His sheaf stoop up straight, but their sheaves bowed down to his. When he told his brothers the dream, they immediately felt threatened. They said, "Are you actually going to reign over us?" (Genesis 37:8). They hated him even more because of his dreams.

Let's think about that. Did Joseph say that he would rule over them? No. He merely told them his dream. His brothers were the ones who gave the interpretation, but they were blind to the fact that the dream and interpretation both came from God! They interpreted the dream, but left God out of the picture. The dream ultimately did come to pass and his brothers bowed down to him (see Genesis 42:6).

Whenever you interpret your situation and leave God out of the picture, you will react in the wrong way. To respond correctly, you must by faith see God's hand at work in your situation, even when circumstances look bleak.

You focus on failing instead of succeeding.

Optimists light candles. Pessimists blow them out.

Optimism lifts up. Pessimism pulls down.

Optimists see success. Pessimists focus on failure.

Karl Wallenda of the Flying Wallendas was famous for his tightrope walking. Throughout his career he continually amazed the crowds with his uncanny balance. His life came to an end in 1978 in San Juan, Puerto

Rico, when he plunged to his death while crossing a seventy-five-foot-high cable between two hotels.

When his wife was later asked why he fell, she gave an interesting explanation. "All Karl thought about for three straight months prior to his accident was falling. It was the first time he had ever thought about that, and it seemed to me that he put all his energies into not falling rather than walking the tightrope."

Wallenda slipped because his focus was on falling. For the last three months of his life, he took a pessimist's view of tightrope walking. While many people affirm the power of positive thinking, few people grasp the destructive power of negative thinking.

If a boxer thinks that he will lose the fight, he will. If a football team believes it will lose, they won't win, no matter how talented they may be. If you keep thinking that your marriage is going to fail, it eventually will.

Instead of thinking negatively, why don't you include God in your situation and ask Him to intervene? With the Lord involved, you can now begin to think positively.

Don't let the fear of falling control your thinking. As you walk over the tightrope of life, keep your eyes fixed on Jesus. He will lead you with assurance to the other side.

You frequently complain.

Pessimists are known to gripe about everything because they always focus on what's wrong instead of what's right.

A new arrival in heaven was surprised to see a suggestion box along Main Street. He asked an angel standing nearby, "If everyone is happy in heaven, why is there a suggestion box here?"

The angel replied, "Because some people aren't happy unless they're complaining."

A pessimistic perspective on life always produces grumbling. I can't find any verse in the Bible that says the Lord will bless whining. Complaining is a verbalization of a negative attitude, which takes away your ability to enjoy God's blessings.

My wife and I celebrated our twenty-fifth wedding anniversary by taking a cruise for the first time in our lives. We were amazed at how the crew members waited on us like we were royalty. We thoroughly enjoyed eating the gourmet food, watching the entertainment shows each evening, and visiting the beautiful islands. We were so thankful that God would let us go on the trip of lifetime.

One day, all the passengers had to go to a certain place on the ship where we waited to disembark. As everyone was waiting in line, something caused a delay. After thirty minutes passed, a grouchy man yelled in anger, "This is the worst cruise I've ever been on. I can't believe how bad the service is!"

Immediately a woman with a look of disgust on her face shouted, "You can say that again! I've been on cruises much better than this."

I turned to my wife and said, "Are we on the same boat as those two? Here we are in the lap of luxury, away from work, eating the finest food, the service is fantastic, on the trip of a lifetime—and all they can do is find something to gripe about!"

The problem wasn't the food on the ship, or the service on the ship, or the entertainment on the ship, but the pessimism in their hearts.

Becoming a Biblical Optimist

What's the difference between an optimist and a biblical optimist? Both think positively, but a biblical optimist sees God's hand working in all situations and trusts His promises. In other words, a Christian can have a positive outlook on life due to the "God Factor." It's not just wishful thinking, but a spiritual reality.

An optimistic attitude comes from disciplining your mind. You've got to think about what you're thinking about. You're filtering your thoughts—rejecting the negative ones and accepting uplifting ones. "But examine everything carefully; hold fast to that which is good" (1 Thessalonians 5:21). To "change your mind" involves two disciplines.

1. Focus on what's good in your situation.

Edith and Shirley were having coffee one morning. Shirley looked out the window and was awestruck by the sun shining on the flower garden. "Wow, it's beautiful out there!" she said.

"Yeah," Edith replied, "but look at all the dirt on the window."

Which do you see? The dirt on the window or the flowers in the garden?

You can't get rid of pessimism without changing the way you think. You've got to deprogram your mind from the negative thinking and then reprogram it with positive thoughts. Changing your attitude requires an act of your will.

One day a little girl whined about everything from the time she woke up until she went to bed that night. The next day she was in a cheerful mood all day. Her mother asked, "Why are you so happy today? Yesterday you had a horrible attitude."

"Yesterday my thoughts pushed me around," she said, "but today I decided to push them around."

The apostle Paul, the ultimate biblical optimist, knew how to push around his thoughts. "Finally, brethren, whatever is true, whatever is honorable, whatever is right, whatever is pure, whatever is lovely, whatever is of good repute, if there is any excellence and if anything worthy of praise, *dwell on these things*" (Philippians 4:8).

When a sponge is full of water, it can't absorb any more because it's saturated. When your mind is saturated with godly thoughts, you won't absorb pessimistic ideas. As long as you keep filling your mind with uplifting thoughts, you'll have peace. But if you start feeling sorry for yourself and gripe about how life is unfair, you'll exchange your joy for torment. Think about it. Is it worth it?

A number of years ago my wife, Cindy, refueled our car at a filling station in Texas. Since she had never been there before, she accidentally pulled up to a full-service pump instead of the self-service pump. She didn't realize the luxury service cost an extra fifty cents per gallon until she paid for the gas.

Later, when she told me about how much the station charged for full service, I got mad. *That extra fifty cents per gallon surely has to be a violation of some federal law*, I thought. I quickly calculated that the extra seven dollars she paid for full service would have taken our vehicle 128.33 miles farther down the road if she had bought self-service gas. The "full-service gas station robbery" rubbed me the wrong way.

As I was mulling over this injustice, God showed me what I had done. He spoke to my heart, "You've just sold your joy for seven dollars!" I never thought about how cheaply I would trade off something so valuable. Just as Esau sold off his birthright for a bowl of soup, I exchanged my joy for a few dollars' worth of gas.

God used that incident to teach me a valuable lesson. How many other times have I lost my joy by focusing on little grievances that don't really matter? I decided right then that I wouldn't forfeit my happiness so easily again. My joy is too precious to allow the thief of pessimism to pickpocket it.

Imagine going on a picnic. The weather's perfect and everyone is having a great time, but a fly keeps buzzing around you. Now instead of enjoying the day, you're focusing on the fly. You keep trying to swat it, missing every time. It continues to bother you, and rest of the afternoon you're focused on the fly instead of the picnic. The "fly at the picnic" has just ruined your day!

What is the "fly" that's stealing your joy? At what price are you willing to give up your happiness? It may be someone pulling in front of you on the highway, or a small incident at work. It could be a misplaced remote control, a flat tire, or someone's smart-aleck words directed at you.

Don't fall into the fly-trap. Don't let those little aggravating things in life steal the joy that God wants you to have.

2. *Stop complaining and start thanking.*

The quickest way to kill the giant of pessimism is with the weapon of thankfulness. Quit complaining. "Do everything without complaining" (Philippians 2:14 NLT). That's hard to do.

I once decided that I wanted to go the rest of my life without complaining. I realized that it's possible to gripe without realizing it, so I asked for my wife's assistance. "Honey," I said, "I want to go the rest of my life without complaining. If you should ever hear me gripe, I want you to raise your finger in the air as a signal to me."

Later that day I saw her holding up her finger.

"What are you doing?" I asked.

"You told me to hold it up if you griped. You just complained about something."

It stunned me how quickly I had failed. I wanted to go the rest of my life but couldn't even make it through the day! It's not that easy to quit the habit of negative talking. It's something I have to stay on top of every day. But I knew if I would start thanking God for everything, my complaining would automatically cease. I can't be thankful and complain at the same time.

Paul instructed, "In everything give thanks; for this is God's will for you in Christ Jesus" (1 Thessalonians 5:18). Thanking the Lord when things aren't going well is a statement of faith, declaring that you believe God is in control. Every time you thank Him, you acknowledge your trust in Him despite what you see.

Being optimistic doesn't mean to ignore reality, but to purposely look for the best in every situation and then thank the Lord for it. Instead of complaining about the price of gasoline, give thanks to God that you can still get it. Rather than griping about your job, be thankful that you have employment.

I knew a man who hated his job and constantly complained, even though it paid him well. When he lost his job, he went into shock. He told me, "Where am I going to find a job that pays as well as this one?" Perhaps he would not have been fired if he had been thankful every day instead of wearing down his fellow employees with his whining.

Thankfulness has the incredible power to turn our attitude around. God wants us to hunt for treasure, even in bad situations. We can always find something positive in our current situation if we'll look for it.

I know what you're thinking. How can Roy Parrino find treasure in his occupation? How is it possible to be an optimist when you're working in a sewer?

The first day on the job, Roy descended into his "big toilet" and emerged holding a two-carat topaz ring. Parrino has found necklaces, bracelets, and diamond rings while working in sewers. Even in his disgusting environment, Roy doesn't focus on filth because he's too busy hunting for diamonds.

You can also discover treasure in your current situation. No matter how horrible your circumstances may appear, a hidden jewel is buried beneath and calls out for you to find it.

So the next time you're up to your neck in problems, just remember one thing. You can find diamonds in a sewer if you'll look for them.

Chapter 12

ANGER

Anger Mismanagement

> And He found in the temple those who were selling oxen and
> sheep and doves, and the money changers seated at their tables.
> And He made a scourge of cords, and drove them all out of
> temple. (John 2:14–15)

It was the best of times; it was the worst of times. The temple in Jerusalem, which was dedicated as a place of holy worship, had turned into a business center. The animals to be offered as sacrifices were being sold for a healthy profit. The money changers had set up their own lucrative business as bankers, exchanging foreign currency for Hebrew shekels. It was the best of times if you wanted to make a quick buck.

Imagine how Jesus must have felt when He walked into the temple court and watched the people haggling over the prices of animals. He sees the money changers, who couldn't care less about worshipping God, counting their stacks of coins. Their greedy little hands pushed His hot button! The same Jesus who kissed babies was about to show them His angry side.

He grabbed some ropes, made a makeshift whip, turned over their tables, and drove the money changers out of the temple courtyard. It was the worst of times for the spiritual state of Israel.

Anger in itself is not sinful. Otherwise, Jesus would have committed His first sin when He did this. Because He never sinned, His anger was both holy and justified. I wish I could say the same thing for every time we get angry.

Do you understand what causes anger? We get angry when others do something that we don't want them to do, or they aren't doing something that we do want them to do. Someone is not meeting our expectations.

For example, a father tells his daughter to clean her room. Later that day he sees the room hasn't been cleaned. He gets mad because she *didn't do* what he wanted (clean her room), so he grounds her for the weekend. Now she gets mad at him because he did something that she *didn't want* him to do (grounding her).

Husbands and wives get mad at each other because their expectations aren't met. They blame each other for what they are, or aren't, doing. The problem multiplies when they keep fighting over the same issues again and again.

We can also get angry when circumstances aren't going the way we would like. What we want to happen and what's actually happening are not matching up. Again, our expectations aren't being met.

We get mad at God because we want Him to do something, but He doesn't obey our wishes. Jonah was furious with God when He didn't wipe the people of Nineveh off the map (see Jonah 4:1). And if He hasn't answered our prayers by our designated deadline, we get upset at Him. Who does He think He is, anyway? We think, *Boy, if I could just have five minutes to govern the universe, I could show God a thing or two about how to fix this place!*

Tell-Tale Signs of Sinful Anger

You know you're angry when the temperature in the room goes up fifteen degrees and no one has touched the thermostat. Although anger is not necessarily sinful, it can quickly turn into sin if we mismanage it. Here are three telltale signs that show when anger turns into sin.

Anger turns into sin when it's out of control.

In seven different books in the Old Testament, it specifically says that God is slow to anger. In contrast, Galatians 5:20 describes one of the works of the flesh as "outbursts of anger." This describes a person who quickly explodes when something doesn't go his way.

Anger is usually manifested in a couple of ways. It can *explode* through lashing out at others, or it can *implode* inside you when you push it down and stuff it. Explosive anger is like throwing a hand grenade at someone, which maims the intended target. Implosive anger is like setting a trash can on fire and then sticking it in a closet. It doesn't solve your problem, but only hides it.

What does it take to set you off? Someone once said you can measure a man by the size of whatever it takes to make him mad. Hot-tempered anger often creates consequences that lead to regrets.

A man from Philadelphia killed a driver who cut in front of him on the expressway. The traffic on the freeway had slowed down and was being funneled into a single lane. The man had been waiting fifteen minutes to enter the flow of traffic when another car passed on the shoulder of the highway and cut in front of his car. Then the other driver laughed and made an obscene gesture at him.

It was too much for the man. When the traffic stopped, he took a gun out of his glove compartment, got out of the car, walked up to the side of the car of the man who had taunted him, and shot him to death.[1]

E. Stanley Jones, the well-known missionary to India, once observed, "Actions have killed its thousands but reactions its ten thousands." The one who angers you controls you. We can "kill" people, spiritually speaking, by venting our hostility on others. If you explode in outbursts of anger, it is proof that you have no self-control.

Self-control means you are submitted to the Holy Spirit, which is one of the evidences that He is controlling your life (see Galatians 5:23). Proverbs 16:32 says, "He who is slow to anger is better than the mighty, / And he who rules his spirit, than he who captures a city." This verse tells us ruling our own spirits is more important than ruling over an entire city. Some people have power and authority over millions of people but have no control over their own spirit. I won't mention any politicians by name.

Alexander the Great, the commander of the Greek Empire, conquered the known world. After he had accomplished this feat, he went into his tent weeping and cried out, "There are no more worlds to conquer."

On one occasion, Cleitus, a dear friend of Alexander and a general in his army, got drunk and ridiculed the emperor in front of his men. Alexander, seized with anger, snatched a spear from the hand of a soldier and hurled it at Cleitus. He intended only to scare him, but the spear hit him and took the life of his childhood friend.

Alexander instantly regretted what he had done, but it was too late. Overcome with guilt, he attempted to take his own life with the same spear, but was stopped by his men. For days he lay sick, calling for his friend Cleitus whom he had murdered. Alexander the Great had conquered many cities and countries, but he had failed to conquer his own spirit.

Take a moment right now and ask yourself if you are in control your spirit, or if anger is ruling your life.

Anger becomes sin when it isn't resolved quickly.

The apostle Paul said, "Be angry, and yet do not sin; do not let the sun go down on your anger, and do not give the devil an opportunity" (Ephesians 4:26–27). Pastor John Piper has said, "Harbored anger is the only thing the Bible explicitly says opens a door and invites the devil in."

Some time ago, a man went camping in Glacier National Park in Montana. Campers should never take food into their tent because the smell attracts bears. This man caught some fish one evening and wanted to cook them for breakfast, so he brought them into his tent for the night. Sure enough, the bears smelled the fish, which invited them into the tent—and had *him* for supper.

You don't want to invite the bears into your tent, and you don't want to invite the devil into your life. When you hold on to anger without resolving it, you are opening a door and inviting Satan to attack you.

"Do not let the sun go down on your anger" means we must resolve it before the day is over. Comedian Phyllis Diller once said, "Don't go to bed angry. Stay up and fight." But this verse doesn't mean to get in as many punches as possible before the sun goes down. It means to do everything possible to settle the situation that day. If your anger is prolonged for just two days, it has turned into sin.

Something happens to us when we are angry for more than one day. We push our anger down into the soil of our hearts, where it sits in darkness. This two-day-old anger then turns into the seed of unforgiveness. As we nurture the seed of unforgiveness in the soil of our hearts, it sprouts into the root of bitterness.

Scripture gives this warning: "See to it that no one comes short of the grace of God; that no root of bitterness springing up causes trouble, and by it many be defiled" (Hebrews 12:15). Author John Powell has said, "When I repress my emotions, my stomach keeps score." It won't be long before we feel turbulence inside our stomachs.

Suppose a doctor came to you with a ball of torment that was churning, twisting, and looking terrible. He says, "I will pay you $1,000 per day if I can operate on you, cut you open, and implant this ball of turmoil inside. You will lose all of your peace and joy, and the only thing you will be able to think about all day and night is this torment inside of you. Well, how about it?"

You'd say, "It's not worth $1,000 per day to carry that ball of torment inside. As a matter of fact, I wouldn't carry it for all the money in the world." But whenever we hold on to our anger, which eventually turns into bitterness, we're saying, "I'll carry that ball of turmoil inside of me free of charge."

Don't let your anger turn into bitterness. You will pay dearly for it. Resolve it quickly, for your own sake.

Anger turns into sin when it's not mixed with grief.

Jesus was about to heal a man's withered hand on the Sabbath. The Pharisees were watching and ready to condemn Him if He performed the miracle. Jesus looked at them "with anger, grieved at their hardness of heart" (Mark 3:5). He looked past their flesh and bones directly into their hearts. His anger was in response to their stubborn, rebellious attitudes.

Notice the two emotions mentioned in this verse. Jesus looked at them with anger, but He was also *grieved*. Anger needs to be combined with grief to keep it healthy. A degree of sorrow was mixed in with His anger. If grief had not accompanied Jesus' anger, He would have been like Clint Eastwood holding the gun on the criminal and saying, "Go ahead, punk. Make my day!"

Jesus took no pleasure in His anger. Since His anger was mixed with grief, it was as if He were saying, "Why don't you guys open your eyes and soften your hearts?" He wanted them to change so He wouldn't have to be angry with them. Although the Pharisees plotted to kill Him, He still loved them and wanted them to come to repentance.

You've probably heard the expression, "Hate the sin, but love the sinner." We've quoted it so often but have forgotten how to practice it. But it really is a truthful statement. We must learn to direct our anger against the wrong attitudes and not the person. When a doctor is operating on a patient to remove a cancerous tumor, the doctor hates the tumor but loves the patient. Just as Jesus did, we should direct our anger and grief at their stubborn hearts and not make the people themselves our targets.

Conquering the Giant of Anger

You don't need to attend an "Anger Management" class if you'll just apply the advice given below.

1. *Find the cause of your anger.*

The first step in solving any problem is to figure out what's causing it. A mechanic has to find what's causing the car to malfunction before he can repair it. A doctor has to diagnose the health problem before he or she can treat it. And you have to figure out what's causing you to be angry.

Anger is always caused by something. Suppose you look out the window and see someone with a hammer pounding on your new car. He smashes your windshield and dents your hood. You are outraged as you watch him demolish your car. A few minutes before this you were perfectly calm, but now you're furious because he's doing something that you don't want him to do. The damage your car sustains (the wound you receive) makes you angry at the person doing the harm to your property.

Cain and Abel both brought offerings to God. The Lord received Abel's offering but not Cain's, which made Cain mad (see Genesis 4:5). God asked Cain, "Why are you angry? And why has your countenance fallen?" (Genesis 4:6) He wanted Cain to look inside his own heart to find out what caused him to be mad.

Cain had not murdered Abel yet, but God knew what was going to happen if he didn't get rid of his anger. Unchecked anger can lead to murder, and so he warned Cain that "sin is crouching at the door" (Genesis 4:7).

God asks you the same question, "*Why* are you angry?" Stop for a moment and think it through. Are you upset because you are jealous? Is it because you think others should show you more respect? Do you have too many expectations of others?

Before you vent your anger, take a look within. Cain could have said to himself, "Wait a minute. I'm angry. It isn't because of Abel, but because something's wrong in my own heart."

2. *Lower your expectations of others.*

Imagine being a pole-vaulter trying to please your coach. The highest you've been able to clear is thirteen feet. Your coach thinks he's trying to help by pushing you to the limit, so he sets the bar at seventeen feet. When you keep going four feet under the bar, he gets mad and screams at you, using derogatory names. Now you're mad at him because he doesn't understand that the goals he has set are totally unreachable.

A perfectionist is like that coach who sees everyone as a pole-vaulter. He sets the bar so high that no one will ever go over it, no matter how many attempts are made. The root of the problem isn't really with others, but the perfectionist's unrealistic expectations of them. Could it be that the source of your anger problem isn't with the other person, but with you because you've set the bar too high?

A perfectionist wants to control everyone's behavior, thinking that if he can get everyone to obey him, then he'll be happy. He's like the circus person who trains a bear to ride a bicycle. The bear feels awkward doing it, and he's only pedaling because of the trainer's threats. Garrison Keillor once said, "A bear riding a bicycle can be trained to do it, but he would rather be in the woods, doing what bears do."

When I was a kid growing up in New Orleans, our neighborhood had a baseball diamond, where a father would often practice with his son. The dad would hurl fastballs at his twelve-year-old, who was trying to hit them. I figured the father must have played in the pros because his throws were twice as fast as what kids our age were used to. Amazingly his son would hit many of his pitches. But when he missed, his dad would curse loudly at him, and then he'd run over and start beating on his son. I can still picture the boy pleading for him to stop hitting.

The dad would then go back to the pitching mound and yell, "You had better not miss this next one!" This happened on more than one occasion. The perfectionist father was trying to turn his son into a major-league player. I'm sure he never thought of himself as a child abuser but as someone who was just trying to bring out "excellence" in his son. The father set the bar for his son much too high and became furious whenever he failed.

Many times we're angry because we're too hard on other people. If we would lower our expectations so that they aren't unrealistic, our anger would subside. Much of our anger will dissipate if we will humble ourselves and become a servant to others.

Jesus said, "Whoever wishes to become great among you shall be your servant; and whoever wishes to be first among you shall be a slave of all" (Mark 10:43–44). He also said, "Whoever exalts himself shall be humbled; and whoever humbles himself shall be exalted" (Matthew 23:12). Humble servants rarely get angry, because they see their circumstances from a different viewpoint. On the other hand, proud people often get mad at others.

As long as we excuse our anger by blaming others, our problem will remain. We must admit that anger is controlling us and that we need to adjust our attitudes.

3. *Choose to respond in the right way, not the wrong way.*

A rattlesnake in a cage doesn't rattle if it is left alone. But if you poke the snake with a stick, it will rattle and coil as it gets ready to strike back. It has been provoked to anger. When many people are provoked, they react wrongly by striking back. A better way to respond would be to follow Jesus' advice and turn the other cheek (Matthew 5:39).

When you're angry, you can respond in the wrong way or in the right way. After God pointed out Cain's anger, he told him, "If you do what is right, will you not be accepted?" (Genesis 4:7 NIV). We don't know all the details about Cain and Abel's offerings except that God accepted Abel's offering, but He didn't accept Cain's. No doubt his heart wasn't right when he presented his offering.

In several places in the Old Testament, when God approved of an offering, He sent fire to consume it. Perhaps that's how Abel's offering was accepted. Maybe God told Cain if he would go back and give his offering in the right way, it would be accepted just like Abel's.

Cain could have said, "God is giving me another chance to present my offering. Instead of holding a grudge against my brother, I'll do something positive. This time I'll joyfully give my best offering with faith that God will accept it." If he had done that, fire probably would have come from heaven, and he would have known that God approved it.

Then God gave him a warning, "But if you do not do what is right, sin is crouching at your door; it desires to have you, but you must rule over it" (Genesis 4:7 NIV). He was telling him, "Cain, if you don't get control of your anger, it's going to get you into big trouble."

The Hebrew word for "crouching" describes an animal getting ready to pounce on its victim to kill it. That's how mountain lions attack. I used to have a cat that hunted lizards. When she saw a lizard in the grass, she would slowly creep up to it, get in a crouching position, and then would pounce on it.

God could see how close Cain was to committing murder. He said, "Cain, sin has crept up on you, and now it's in the crouching position. If you don't respond in the right way, it's going to pounce you." Uncontrolled anger opens the door for Satan to attack.

Instead of overreacting, ask the Lord to show you a better way to respond. Lowering your tone of voice would be a good place to start. "A gentle answer turns away wrath, / But a harsh word stirs up anger" (Proverbs 15:1). God will show you how to deal with your situation.

When we moved from Kansas to Georgia, my new job required me to start work before I could get my family moved. My wife stayed behind and cleaned out the house, getting rid of many things in the process.

After we got settled in Georgia, I couldn't find several items I had been looking for. One of those things was a carved wooden elephant that my mother had given to me. For some reason I've always liked elephants, and I really enjoyed this statue because of its remarkable detail.

I said, "Honey, have you seen my wooden elephant? I can't find it anywhere."

I could tell by her reaction that she didn't want to answer. Finally she said, "Well, uh, I sold it in the garage sale. I didn't think you wanted it."

"You *what*?" I said in disbelief. "You sold my elephant in a garage sale? I loved that elephant! Why did you do that?" I had never seen anything quite like it, and I knew it couldn't be replaced.

In moments like this, God can speak unexpectedly, and in this case He did. He said, "Why don't you give the elephant to Me?"

"Because I don't have it anymore," I answered. "How can I give it to You if I don't have it?"

God said, "It's still in your heart. You can offer it to Me as a gift."

I had never thought of that before. And so I did. I prayed, "Lord, I want to give You the wooden elephant as an offering. I don't own it anymore, but it's still in my heart, and I give it to You. It's Yours, and I won't ask for it back. Amen."

Immediately my anger subsided. How could I be mad about something that I had placed in God's hands as a gift? I realized that I had discovered a truth that I could share with others. Since then, I've shared this experience with others who were upset over things they couldn't recover. Just offer it to God as an offering.

Not long after this, I was in a store and spotted a miniature elephant, about the same size as my wooden one. I felt as though God wanted to replace the one I had given up, and since it was only fifteen dollars, I bought it. Sometimes, if you'll react in the right way and do what God says, He will find a way to make it up to you.

4. Accept the fact that you can't change some things.

Football fans often get mad about a call made by a referee. If it's the right call, even if it goes against the team I'm pulling for, I'm okay with that. But it's easy for me to get upset when the ref makes a bad call that costs my team the game. I know people who are still boiling over a referee's call from years ago.

Is it possible for them to go back in time and change the ref's call? No. Can they alter the outcome of the game? No. Have they lost their joy? Yes.

Many times we get angry over things that we can't change and are completely out of our control. Years ago I used to get angry watching the national news every night. I gritted my teeth at the stupid decisions the government made. When the media put their own slant on reporting the news, it made me boil. I thought my anger against these evil things was the righteousness of God in me.

One day I read James 1:20, "For the anger of man does not achieve the righteousness of God." I had read it many times before, but this time it jumped out at me, like a new revelation. It was as if God were saying to me, "Your anger toward things you can't change isn't accomplishing anything good, but it is taking away your joy."

It made me realize that I was angry about things that I couldn't do anything about. I decided right then that I wasn't going to let the things that I couldn't change eat me up inside anymore. If I couldn't change my circumstances, I would accept them as a fact of life outside my sphere of influence.

By acceptance, I am not talking about putting your stamp of approval on whatever it is that's making you mad. It just means that if you can't do anything about it, then choose to be happy anyway. Many things that happen are neither good nor right, and we certainly would prevent them from occurring if it were possible. Events in our past can't be altered, no matter how much we may wish we could change them. Some people, whom we once knew, we will never see again. We may never have an opportunity to clear up unresolved differences with them. Many events happen on a national and international level that we can do nothing about, except to watch them take place.

In these cases, you must accept the fact that this is the way it is, and you can do nothing to change the outcome. If you don't accept the fact that you can't change things beyond your control, you will stay angry for the rest of your life. Doesn't it make more sense to find ways to be happy instead of frustrated?

5. *Divorce yourself from anger.*

In the movie *Forrest Gump*, Jenny, Forrest's love since childhood, returned to her old home after her father died. The old farm house was dilapidated and abandoned. As she reflected on the sexual abuse she endured as a child, she was overcome with rage and angrily threw rocks at the house. Jenny went out of control as she repeatedly picked up rocks and threw them. Finally she fell to the ground in exhaustion. Forrest commented on the incident by saying, "Sometimes there just aren't enough rocks."

Jenny identified the cause of her anger, but she didn't know how to remove it. Throwing rocks doesn't fix the problem. God's Word tells us, "Let all bitterness and wrath and anger and clamor and slander be put away from you, along with all malice. Be kind to one another, tender-hearted, forgiving each other, just as God in Christ also has forgiven you" (Ephesians 4:31–32). Malice is the anger that wants to harm the person who has hurt us.

To "put away" means "to divorce." Paul says, "You need to get a divorce—not from your spouse, but from your anger and bitterness." You can divorce yourself from anger by saying, "I'm not married to you anymore. You've got to leave and not come back!" Maybe if more people divorced themselves from their anger, there would be less divorce.

We must get a divorce from all bitterness, wrath, and anger. God never commands us to do something we aren't capable of doing. The real issue, then, is our willingness to remove it from our lives. When we remove garbage from our house, we make a decision to carry it out of the house to the trash receptacle and release it there. The first thing we must do is to make a decision that we want it gone and out of our lives.

A surgeon named Dr. Kane searched for a candidate to undergo surgery so he could prove that appendectomies could be done under local anesthetic. At last a patient was found. He was prepared for surgery and wheeled into the operating room. A local anesthetic was applied, leaving the patient able to talk and respond as the surgery progressed.

As he had done hundreds of times, Dr. Kane located the appendix, skillfully removed it, and finished the surgery. During the operation the patient complained only of minor discomfort. He was taken to a hospital room, recovered quickly, and was dismissed two days later. Dr. Kane had demonstrated that local anesthesia was a viable and sometimes preferable alternative, thanks to the willingness of a brave volunteer.

What I didn't tell you was that the courageous volunteer for surgery by Dr. Kane—was Dr. Kane. He had performed surgery upon himself and removed his own appendix![2]

Sometimes the surgery you need can only be performed by yourself, on yourself. You can't wait for someone else to remove your anger and bitterness for you. You must remove and release it yourself.

My wife and I have been happily married for thirty-five years. We enjoy spending time together because we are best friends. However, years ago I was slowly building up anger against her. I found things wrong with what she did, even when she hadn't done anything wrong. I thought she was the problem until I was praying one morning and God nailed me. The words came into my mind, "You are angry with Cindy."

Immediately I was convicted of my judgmental attitude—to which I had been blind. The Lord showed me that I needed to perform spiritual heart surgery and remove my cancerous attitude. I felt so ashamed of my critical attitude that I cried before the Lord for about an hour.

During this hour of purging, God showed me that I had picked up this anger from my father. He was often mad at my mother and critical about one thing or another. The Bible talks about the iniquity of the fathers visiting their children to the third and fourth generations (see Exodus 20:5; Numbers 14:18; Psalm 106:6). We often become like our parents because we tend to copy their behavior, and we'll pick up their iniquities unless we choose to stop the cycle.

I prayed, "Lord, I'm breaking that generational curse. I'm not going to let the anger of my father rule my life anymore. I am not going to treat my wife with harshness. I repent and I ask You to forgive me." I asked Cindy to forgive me, which she did.

I can honestly tell you that something huge left me that day. I don't have any doubt I was delivered from a spirit of anger. That doesn't mean I've never been angry since then, but about 95 percent of the things I was angry about no longer bother me.

Anger and bitterness are usually a result of a past hurt. Unhealed wounds cause us to become angry, and unresolved anger leads to unforgiveness and bitterness. When you forgive those who have hurt you, you reverse the process. Forgiving frees you to remove your feelings of anger, and removing the anger allows God to heal your wounds from the past.

To remove your anger, you've got to perform heart surgery on yourself. No one can do it for you. This is one divorce that God encourages. Repent of unrighteous anger. Forgive those who have hurt you. Ask forgiveness. Replace your harshness with kindness and a tender heart (Ephesians 4:32) and learn to make the best out of life.

A boy was skating down the road on one skate. A man saw him and asked, "Why are you on one skate? Don't you know you're supposed to skate on two skates?"

The boy answered, "Well, mister, someone stole my other skate, and that's why I'm skating on one."

After the man walked away, the boy yelled to him, "Hey, mister, did you know that you can still have a lot of fun on just one skate?"

Make the most of your situation. You can get mad at the person who stole your skate, or you can keep having fun on the one skate you have left. It's your choice.

Chapter 13

REJECTION

The Angel Inside the Marble

"If the world hates you, you know that it has hated Me before it hated you." (John 15:18)

The Italian sculptor Michelangelo stared at a block of marble that had been rejected by another artist. A friend approached him and asked what he was looking at.

Michelangelo replied, "An angel."

He was able to see what others couldn't and chiseled an angel out of the stone that another sculptor had rejected.

Two thousand years ago, Jesus Christ was also a rejected stone.

"The stone which the builders rejected,
This became the chief corner stone;
This came about from the Lord,
And it is marvelous in our eyes." (Matthew 21:42)

From the Lord? Marvelous? Not the rejection. The other part of the verse: "This became the chief cornerstone." Although men hated Jesus and wanted nothing to do with Him, His Father chiseled Him into the foundation for the Church. What enemies plan for evil, God intends for good. The heavenly Father fashioned the rejected Messiah into the world's Savior.

Sure, that's true for Christ. But what about when *we* are rejected? Can God chisel an angel out of the marble for us? If we could always see God's hand sculpturing our lives, that would truly be "marvelous in our eyes" as well.

Rejection isn't what happens to us, but *how we interpret* what happens to us. It's how we view ourselves in relation to others. Are we so insecure that we can't handle being spurned? Some people are devastated when they aren't accepted.

A young salesman became discouraged because he had been rejected by so many customers he approached. He asked a more experienced salesman for some advice.

"Why is it, every time I make a call on someone that I get rejected?"

"I just don't understand it," answered the older salesman. "I've been hit on the head, called dirty names, and thrown out the door, but I've never been rejected."

Life would be so much easier if we could find an effective way to deal with people's rejection. In spite of all the hatred that Jesus received, He chose not to be offended. He was only interested in pleasing His Father and always trusted Him to control the outcome.

We always respond to others according to how we perceive a situation. If we are easily offended, it's highly likely that we will think people are avoiding us, even if they aren't. Single people sometimes think that no one on the planet could possibly love them enough to marry them. This false belief—the "no one will love me" syndrome—leaves God completely out of the picture. It can even build unnecessary barriers, which actually create more rejection.

Sources of Rejection

Because fellowship is built upon acceptance, rejection is the main enemy to establishing healthy relationships. Rejection usually comes from three sources.

REJECTION

Rejection through "difficult people"

Just because someone rejects you doesn't mean the problem is with you. The problem may be with a dysfunctional person who makes everyone feel incompetent.

When Jimmy came home from school, his mother asked, "How do you like your new teacher?"

"She's mean, but she's fair," Jimmy replied.

"What do you mean by that?"

"Well, she's mean, but she's mean to everyone."

Some people are mean to everyone. I call them *difficult people* because they make life hard on others. Since the world contains a high percentage of these impolite individuals, your chances of encountering one are pretty good. Don't take their snubbing as a personal insult. These irrational people are mean to everyone, not just you. They don't know how to kindly respond to others.

You have a choice. You can accept their rejection, or you can reject it. If you invite rejection into your heart, you will feel unwanted, unloved, and unworthy. But if you will refuse to let them bother you, you'll go about your business with peace in your heart.

When Elizabeth Barrett became the wife of poet Robert Browning, her parents disowned her because they disapproved of the marriage. She continued to write her mother and father regularly for years, telling them how much she loved them.

Elizabeth never received a response from her parents until ten years later, when she received a huge package in the mail. She eagerly opened the box only to discover it contained every letter she had sent them for a decade—all unopened. Although she wanted to be reunited with her parents, they refused to accept her in spite of her many attempts.[1]

Difficult people actually receive satisfaction through rejecting others. In a morbid sort of way, they try to punish others by their snubbing. Does that mean you are destined to a life of unworthiness because you can't gain their approval? Of course not. God has called us to freedom, not bondage (see Galatians 5:13).

No matter what happens, don't let rude people make you feel unacceptable. Find your acceptance through your relationship with Christ and not through trying to appease someone who cannot be pleased.

Rejection through ourselves

Some people never realize that they themselves are the source of their own rejection. The pastor of a large congregation in Dallas told me about his friend who had visited his church. His friend told the pastor that he wanted to measure the church's friendliness. "I'll stand in the foyer of your church, and I'm almost certain that no one will shake my hand."

The pastor replied, "We have a friendly church. I know that our members will greet you."

After the church service, his friend stood in the foyer as hundreds of people walked past him. After everyone had left, the pastor asked, "Well, did anyone shake your hand?"

"Not a single person."

The pastor was dumbfounded. "What did you do? You must have done something to keep them from meeting you."

His friend explained that he performed an experiment. "Every time someone started to approach me, I simply looked away and gave the impression I didn't want to meet them. They could sense I was rejecting them, so they turned and walked away."

This man demonstrated why some people never form close friendships. They initiate their own rejection by rolling out an *unwelcome* mat toward others—using gestures like frowning, looking away, crossing arms, or staring at the floor. If this man had warmly smiled at those approaching him, he would have met a number of people.

A cold shoulder will sabotage a relationship before it ever gets started. Why would someone want to be your friend if you keep pushing them away with your attitude? Many people don't have a clue they are causing their own rejection, so they get angry when others don't befriend them. They should actually blame themselves for creating barriers that keep others away.

REJECTION

Rejection through imaginations

Highly sensitive people often struggle with imaginations of rejection. Their overly active imaginations create the rejection they love to hate. Rejected people take no for an answer before the question has even been asked. They program their minds to assume that others' responses will always be negative. They look for rejection everywhere—and find it. False imaginations cause them to misinterpret innocent intentions and draw wrong conclusions.

One man described a situation where he imagined that others avoided him. He said, "When I walked into the room, everyone scattered." He assumed their exits were due to his entrance into the room, but that wasn't the case.

The facts came out later. Several people had left the room, but not because he entered it. They had other appointments and needed to leave at that time. Because this man often felt rejected, it was quite easy for him to misinterpret their actions. He read between the lines and filled in the blanks.

Be careful not to interpret others' actions as rejection. Your assumptions may incorrectly judge their intentions. You might believe certain individuals are trying to avoid you when in reality they aren't. You only *think* they are, like this man who believed people exited the room to avoid him.

Imaginations can destroy relationships because they make you assume things that aren't true. I once knew a woman with a history of rejection, who was always suspicious of others' motives. A friend once complimented her, saying, "You sure look nice today."

The woman replied, "Are you saying that I don't look nice every day? You said I look nice *today*. That means you think I don't look good on other days."

Her puzzled friend said, "No, I didn't mean that. I just think the dress that you're wearing looks nice. I didn't mean . . ."

"Well, I don't know how to take it any other way. You think I look bad most of the time, don't you?"

Because of her distorted perspective, this woman turned a compliment into an insult. Do you see how imaginations of rejection can sabotage relationships?

It's hard to convince people who are constantly imagining being rejected that they are truly loved. I heard about a wife who felt undeserving of her husband's love. She had a difficult time believing that anyone, including her husband, could ever love her.

To test his love, she withdrew and tried to get him to reaffirm his acceptance of her. After several episodes of this withdrawal-acceptance cycle, her husband exploded in anger because of her continual need for reassurances. In the wife's mind, his angry reaction confirmed her imaginations—that he was just pretending to love her. She would never be able to receive her husband's acceptance as long as she assumed he didn't really love her.

No amount of affirmation will ever be enough to satisfy the ever-growing demands of someone who views every action as rejection. Only the truth can set a person free from these lying thoughts. Jesus said, "And you will know the truth, and the truth will make you free" (John 8:32).

Don't forfeit your joy any longer.

Defeating the Giant of Rejection

Here are three ways to reject rejection:

1. *Find freedom in God's acceptance of you, not in others' acceptance of you.*

Paul wrote: "Now accept the one who is weak in faith . . . for God has accepted him" (Romans 14:1, 3). Isn't it encouraging knowing that God accepts you even if no one else does? You must accept the fact that God accepts you. Receiving your approval from God will help you overcome the painful rejections of hateful people.

Karen's alcoholic and abusive father abandoned his family when she was two years old. Every Father's Day her mother made her write a card to the father she never knew. Her father never responded. Although

Karen's father never cared for her, she finally found a different way to fill the void. Someone taught her at church that God could be her father.

Whenever she went out to play on her roller skates, she yelled, "Hey God, look at me!" She felt a special awareness of His presence, as if God were smiling from heaven. Instead of focusing her attention on the man who had abandoned her, she directed her affection toward God, who is "a father of the fatherless" (Psalm 68:5). Although she never received approval from her earthly father, Karen found security through her heavenly Father. Today she's a spiritually healthy woman, grounded in the love of God.

Turn your spiritual eyes upward to God instead of focusing on others. As long as you're craving acceptance from people, you'll continue to experience the disappointments of rejection. However, if you will find your approval in Christ, you can rest in His acceptance of you.

2. *View some rejections as closed doors from God.*

Jesus instructed His disciples to shake the dust off their feet when the unwelcome mat was rolled out. He said, "Whoever does not receive you, nor heed your words, as you go out of that house or that city, shake the dust off your feet" (Matthew 10:14). Christ wanted them to move on and leave rejection behind.

That's good advice. Shake off your rejection and look for new opportunities. Don't let even one speck of rejection stick to the soles of your feet, or you will carry it with you to the next village. Don't permit your past rejections to distort your view of future opportunities.

Even though people rejected Jesus, He became the head of the church. God's plan isn't undermined just because you are not warmly welcomed by a few people. Some of your rejections should be viewed as God's way of diverting you to something better.

The first book that I wrote was rejected by fifteen different publishing companies. Rejection letters from publishers can be discouraging, so whenever I received one, I prayed by faith, "Lord, thank You for this rejection letter. This must not be the right company. Please open the right door if You want this published."

One day I received a letter from an editor who loved my manuscript and eventually published my book, which went into several printings and was translated into Korean. God closed doors through those rejection letters to divert me to the right publisher.

Man's rejection can actually be God's direction. Your rejection didn't take God by surprise, just as it didn't shock Him when Joseph's brothers threw him into a pit and sold him into slavery (see Genesis 37). Joseph didn't get angry and bitter at his brothers. Instead, he fully submitted himself to divine providence, knowing that God would use their hateful actions to fulfill His ultimate plan.

Looking past their hateful actions, Joseph saw God's hand at work. Through God's amazing sovereignty, Joseph was eventually promoted from being a slave to holding the second-highest position in Egypt. If Joseph's brothers hadn't rejected him, his promotion would not have happened. Years later, Joseph told his brothers that two plans were at work at the same time, "You meant evil against me, but God meant it for good" (Genesis 50:20).

As horrible as your pit may be or how abandoned you may feel, you have the opportunity to act like Joseph. The people who rejected you truly meant it for evil, but the Lord will use their rejection to get you to a new and better place, where He can bless you.

Choose to view your rejections in a new way. An angel is locked up in that block of marble. God may be protecting you from a harmful relationship. A broken engagement can be the hand of God halting one relationship so He can guide you to His choice. Failure to be hired for a job may mean God is directing you to a different assignment. Submit your decisions to the lordship of Jesus Christ, and He will make sure the wrong doors close and the right doors open in His timing.

3. *Try to be at peace with those who reject you.*

Although you may not become friends with those who reject you, God wants you to make an attempt at peace. "If possible, so far as it depends on you, be at peace with all men" (Romans 12:18). Many times it's not possible, but at least make an attempt. If your attempt fails, you can still have peace of mind even if your enemy won't accept you.

Sometimes *your attempt* to make peace will remove your feelings of rejection. God wants you to obey Him, even if your efforts to make peace fail. You may never be reconciled with someone who holds grudges and refuses to work out differences. However, making this attempt can set you free from your rejection, and it might even soften the hearts of those who dislike you.

I once counseled a man named George, who told me his worst childhood memory was his father holding a knife to his mother's throat, threatening to kill her. He felt the sting of rejection on the day when his dad moved out and abandoned his family. He hated his father and swore he would never be like him. As George grew up, every memory of his dad kindled anger within him. Ironically, the more he thought about his father, the more he became like him.

Forty years later George attended a Promise Keepers' meeting where the topic of discussion was mending father-son relationships. Now that George was a Christian, God tugged at his heart to forgive his father for the terrible things he had done. He wondered how he could ever have a good relationship with a father who had rejected, abused, and abandoned his own family. Perhaps if he made an attempt to be reconciled, God would set him free from his own hatred. However, he didn't even know where his father lived.

George began his search to find the man who had rejected him more than four decades before. He decided that if he found him, he would love him unconditionally. After several months of investigation, his leads took him to a bar in Portland, Oregon. He walked into the tavern and asked the bartender, "Do you know a man named Bill, who is a frequent customer here?" The man pointed to an elderly man sitting at a table by himself.

George pulled up a chair next to the seventy-six-year-old man. He stretched out his hand and introduced himself. "Hi, my name's George."

The old man with the wrinkled face shook his hand, saying, "I have a son named George."

George replied, "I know, Dad. I'm him. How are you doing?"

His father, who had not seen him since he was a boy, choked up with emotion. With tears rolling down his face, he replied in a nervous laugh, "What took you so long to find me?" They hugged and spent the next few hours talking about the past forty years of their lives.

Although he can't explain it, George said all his hatred and rejection left him on that day. He not only made peace with his father, but he also found peace in his own heart by obeying God. He overcame his rejection by accepting his father unconditionally, without demanding that he change to meet his expectations.

Reflecting on this new relationship with his father, George said, "God taught me how to be a father to my son. Now he's teaching me how to be a son to my father."

Don't let rejection get you down. Find your acceptance in God. Remember that closed doors are God's way of keeping you out of trouble. Make peace with everyone, if you can.

And one more thing—look for the angel inside the marble.

Chapter 14

IMPATIENCE

God's Waiting Room

After Abram had lived ten years in the land of Canaan, Abram's wife Sarai took Hagar the Egyptian, her maid, and gave her to her husband Abram as his wife. And he went in to Hagar, and she conceived. . . . Abram was eighty-six years old when Hagar bore Ishmael to him. (Genesis 16:3–4, 16)

When you go to the doctor, the receptionist says, "Please have a seat in the waiting room." Although you're ready to see the doctor, you've got to wait until the doctor is ready to see you. So you're forced to sit in an uncomfortable chair, thumbing through outdated magazines, trying to pass time until the nurse calls your name. Everyone in that room is doing the same thing, and that's why it's called the waiting room.

God also has a waiting room, and Abraham and Sarah had to stay seated a long time before the nurse called their names. Abram, who is better known to us as Abraham, wasn't getting any younger. He was eighty-five years old and had been drawing Social Security for more than two decades. Ten years had passed since God had first promised him he would have a son, but the stork had still not arrived. He had thought about adopting Eliezer to be his heir, but then God told him his heir would come from his own body (Genesis 15:2–4).

So his wife Sarai, whose name was later changed to Sarah, did what most of us do when we get tired of waiting for God to answer our prayers. She decided to figure out a way to fulfill the promise of God. She went to Abram one day with her handmaiden and said in so many words, "Abram, the Lord said the heir would come through your body, but He didn't say anything about my body. Let's use Hagar to fulfill God's promise. I've been barren for years, and I'm tired of waiting for Him to come through. After all, doesn't God expect us to do our part in making things happen?"

So Hagar conceived and gave birth to Ishmael. He was such a cute baby. Little did Abram and Sarai realize that the descendants of that child would be fighting the Jewish people for centuries to come.

Do you ever get tired of waiting for God to answer your prayers? Waiting can be frustrating. One man had a neighbor with a rooster that crowed three times a day, and only three times. The man went to his neighbor and asked him to get rid of it.

The neighbor answered, "He only crows three times a day. Is that too much?"

"No, that isn't too much. But you don't know what I go through waiting to get that third crow over with!"

We are a little like that when we're waiting for God to answer our prayers. We believe He will eventually send an answer, but it drives us crazy not knowing when it will come.

I would rather chop wood than wait. I worked in a drug store when I was in high school. When business was slow, I looked at the clock and it read 1:35. An hour later I'd look at it again and it was 1:45. Ten minutes can seem like an hour when we're ready to clock out.

One afternoon I took my children to the movies. My son Scott, who was seven years old at the time, was anxious for the movie to begin. As the different advertisements appeared on the screen, Scott leaned over and whispered, "Dad, when is the movie going to start?"

"In a few minutes."

One minute later he again asked, "Dad, when is it going to start?"

"In just a little bit."

After he asked the third time, I said, "Scott, don't ask me that question again. Just sit there and wait."

My son, who was a quiet and obedient child, fidgeted and tried to be patient. Finally he leaned over and whispered a different question, "Dad, can you make time go faster?"

My boy didn't have any control over when the movie started, but he thought his father could shorten the waiting period by speeding up time. Many times we say to God, "Father, can You make time go faster? I'm so tired of waiting. I'm ready for my prayer to be answered. Please make it arrive sooner."

Symptoms of Impatience

Are you trying to talk God into speeding up time? The following symptoms reveal impatience.

Symptom 1: *Interfering with God's plan*

Abram and Sarai figured God needed a little help from them. He promised them a son, but He didn't tell them how long they would have to wait for him. Abram probably thought, *I'll only have to wait nine months.* He got out his calendar and started marking off the days. Nine months later Sarai wasn't even showing. Not even a little bulge.

One year passed. Then two. Five years went by. Eight years, then ten. Abram was eighty-five now, and Sarai was at the ripe old age of seventy-five. After a decade of waiting, it was time to do something. They knew God had promised a son, but it was really hard for them to comprehend how a baby could be born from a barren womb.

Then it dawned on them that God needed their help in accomplishing this. Hagar offered her help. Abram offered his help. And Sarai reluctantly offered to stand on the sidelines. We always get into trouble when we try to help out God.

Henry was walking down the street when he saw his neighbor Mr. Smith trying to get a washing machine through the door of his house. He went to the doorway and said, "Here, let me help you." After thirty minutes of struggling with it, Henry said, "I don't think we will ever get this washing machine into the house."

Mr. Smith responded, "Get it in? I'm trying to get it out!"

When we try to help God, we are actually making things harder. Our impatience interferes with God's plan, which can actually cause further delays.

Symptom 2: *Acting impulsively*

The prophet Samuel told King Saul to go to Gilgal and wait seven days until he arrived (see 1 Samuel 10:8; 13:8–12). At that time Samuel would make an offering to the Lord.

Saul went to Gilgal and waited seven days but was growing impatient. The Philistines were getting ready to attack, and his own people were deserting him. As he evaluated the situation, he took matters into his own hands. Figuring he couldn't wait any longer, he acted too quickly and sacrificed the offering himself. He overstepped his boundaries as king and tried to act like a priest.

Wouldn't you know it? At the moment he finished offering the sacrifice, Samuel shows up, and he's not happy one bit about Saul's disobedience. Samuel announces that since he didn't wait for him, God had rejected him as king and was going to find someone else to take his place. Saul thought Samuel was late, but the truth was that his impatience caused him to act irresponsibly.

We grow impatient whenever we think God is delaying. So often we overstep our boundaries and act impulsively, justifying those things in our minds. The Philistines are coming. The people are scattering. Samuel hasn't arrived, so we take matters into our own hands. And we always pay the penalty for acting hastily.

An unmarried person can become impatient. Many singles panic when another birthday passes and they still haven't tied the marriage knot. So they overstep the boundaries and start hunting for a companion in the wrong places, such as bars and questionable websites. Yes, they may well meet someone who is interested in them, but for the wrong reasons. That person may not know God. As a result the lonely single abandons God's plan and hooks up with someone who brings misery and heartache. If you want God's best, you must obey Him and wait for His timing. What God has for you will be worth it.

My brother-in-law married when he was eighteen years old and has had a wonderful marriage for more than thirty years. Another Christian man I know had to wait a lot longer for the right person. When people asked him if he ever wanted to get married, he would say, "Yes, but God hasn't shown me the right person yet." God finally did bring him the right woman, and he married at age thirty-eight. I know another Christian couple; they were singles until they met when they were both forty-nine. All of them received their spouses in God's perfect timing. It's important to be content being single until the Lord makes the match. The Lord loves rewarding those who patiently wait for Him to provide.

Symptom 3: *Becoming restless and irritable*

Sometimes we have a hard time synchronizing our watches with God's will. If we don't rest in the Lord, we become restless. People get on our nerves as we fidget. We might even be on the verge of panic. We expect God quickly to send the answer to our prayer, but He's using the turtle express to deliver it to us. We then assume that God has forgotten about our request, or maybe He just doesn't care. Our frustrations are manifested by our irritable behavior.

We want God's timetable to match ours, rather than ours matching his. We must get to the point where we accept His timing.

Why Should We Wait on the Lord?

The prophet Isaiah tells us that "those who wait for the LORD / Will gain new strength" (Isaiah 40:31). "Waiting on the Lord" means you'll have an *unknown gap of time* between when you call to Him for help and when His answer finally arrives.

God has good reasons for you to wait. Satan always puts his best up front so people will grab it quickly. Those who want instant gratification usually don't wait for God's provision. But the Lord is more concerned about you receiving His best, rather than how quickly you will get it. Doesn't He care about the way you feel? Of course He does, but He has several reasons why He wants you to wait.

Reason 1: *You may not be ready for what God has for you.*

Sometimes waiting periods are designed to prepare you for what God has planned. If you aren't ready for what He has for you, you might not recognize or appreciate the answer when it comes.

My daughter, Hannah, was anxious to drive when she was eleven years old. But I couldn't give her my car keys at that age because she wasn't ready. The car was ready for Hannah, but she wasn't ready for the car. Even though she thought she was ready to drive, I knew better. If she had started driving too soon, she might have been seriously injured in an accident. It wasn't until she turned sixteen and completed a driver's training class that I was able to hand her the keys.

Some people are so anxious to get married, but they aren't ready to make that commitment. They haven't prepared *themselves* to be the best possible mate for their spouse-to-be. Would you want to marry you, as you are right now? Or do you need to make some improvements so that your future spouse will be excited to meet you? Are you in the best physical shape that you can be in? Do you have your financial house in order? Have you corrected your attitudes that keep upsetting others? Now is the time to fix those things, because if you don't change them now, you won't after you get married.

A single person who hasn't properly prepared for marriage is as dangerous as my daughter driving the car at eleven years old. If this describes you, don't let your eagerness to get married blind you to the preparation you need to make. God is waiting for *you* to get ready for what He has planned.

Reason 2: *What God has planned for you may not be ready.*

God may still be in the process of preparing what you are praying for. He may be doing some things "behind the scenes" that you are not aware of. The people, events, and situations involved in God's plan may not yet be in place. You will need to wait for God's perfect timing to bring these things together.

The greatest musicians in the world may come together to play the most beautiful song in the world. But if the musicians' timing is off because they're not watching the conductor, it will sound like total chaos. Timing makes the difference between something being beautiful or annoying.

When the time is right for God to provide, all the players involved will converge together beautifully at the right place. "There is an appointed time for everything" (Ecclesiastes 3:1) and "He has made everything beautiful in its time" (Ecclesiastes 3:11 NASB margin).

Reason 3: *God uses the waiting period to develop patience in you.*

Patience means "to abide under" or "to stand up under pressure." When you begin exercising on a weight-training program, lifting seventy-five pounds might be difficult at first. You may have to struggle to lift that amount of weight over your head. But as you continue to work out, you get stronger, and eventually can lift one hundred pounds. As you continue to make progress, you can then lift 150 pounds over your head. Now anything less than 150 pounds is no longer hard for you, because you've developed the ability to "stand up under pressure."

God uses the waiting periods to develop patience in us so that life actually becomes easier. Abraham grew in strength as he waited all those years (Romans 4:20–21). Patiently waiting on the Lord will not drain one's strength, but will renew it.

Reason 4: *God wants to do a greater miracle for you.*

In John 11 Mary and Martha were in God's Waiting Room after their brother Lazarus had died. If Jesus had come when they had requested, He would have healed Lazarus. But when He didn't show up in time, their brother passed away.

The Scripture points out to us, "Now Jesus loved Martha and her sister and Lazarus" (v. 5). The Holy Spirit made sure these words were recorded for us—that He loved them. While you're sitting in God's Waiting Room, it doesn't look like God loves you. It appears as if He's ignoring you. You're thinking, *Where's God? When is He going to show up? Why is He taking so long? God, don't You care?*

If we're not careful, we can develop some bad theology in the waiting room because nothing seems to be happening. We start believing

God isn't in control. We begin to think He doesn't love us. You can hear Mary and Martha's frustration as they both said, "Lord, if You had been here, my brother would not have died" (vv. 21, 32).

Jesus purposely showed up later because He had something else in mind. By delaying His arrival, He did an even greater miracle by raising Lazarus from the dead. This experience is a lesson for us that God always has a purpose for His delays. Sometimes He is orchestrating events to do something even greater than we expected.

Our church needed to purchase land, and we had prayed for eleven years for God to show us the right place. Over that period of time, the price of land kept escalating. Every piece of property we looked at, God would close the door. We had originally wanted four acres, but as the church grew, we started looking for ten. Land was selling for $45,000 per acre, and we couldn't afford to buy ten acres at that price.

I prayed, "Lord, I know You have some land for us. Please show us where it is."

God immediately put "Eighth Street" in my mind. At first, I wasn't sure if this was God speaking or my own thoughts. But every time I prayed, "Eighth Street" would pop up in my mind. I asked a realtor in our church to check out any property that might be for sale on Eighth Street.

He came back reporting, "A piece of property on Eighth Street just became available this week. People have been trying to buy this land for years, but it hasn't been for sale until now, and we are the first in line. Two land developers also want it, but the owners said will they let us have the first option to buy at a reduced price."

For the eleven years we had been looking for land, this property was not for sale. The moment it opened up, God told us immediately where it was! We bought twenty-two acres of land for $55,000. We had waited a long time for God to provide, and He rewarded us in a greater way than we had ever expected.

How Do We Wait on the Lord?

David knew what it was like to wait on the Lord. He penned the following words of wisdom for all of the future generations, instructing us in how to wait:

Trust in the LORD and do good;
Dwell in the land and cultivate faithfulness.
Delight yourself in the LORD;
And He will give you the desires of your heart.
Commit your way to the LORD,
Trust also in Him, and He will do it. . . .
Rest in the LORD and wait patiently for Him. (Psalm 37:3–5, 7)

Notice the four things he tells us to do when we are waiting.

- *First, trust in the Lord* no matter what the circumstances may look like. He has not forgotten about your request because He is faithful.

- *Second, delight yourself in the Lord.* Have you ever noticed how time flies when you're having fun? Two weeks of vacation seems like two days, while two days of misery seems like two weeks. To delight yourself in the Lord means to find your pleasure in God.

- *Third, commit your way to the Lord.* Jesus committed His spirit into the Father's hands. Committing your way to the Lord means you put your life, your plans, and your future in God's hands.

- *Finally, rest in the Lord* as you patiently wait. Don't worry or fret if everyone else has already received answers to his or her prayers, but you haven't. When you rest, you remove the deadline you've placed on God. All stress is gone. You can't worry when you're resting.

Abraham and Sarah finally lived to see the promised son born. They had been in God's Waiting Room for twenty-five years before the receptionist said, "The doctor will see you now!" Abraham was one hundred years old and Sarah was ninety when she gave birth to Isaac. A quarter century had passed since God first made the promise to them.

Even though your situation may look impossible, just remember that circumstances don't matter to God. Neither does time. All He has to do is speak the word, and it will happen.

So don't jump the gun and do something that you'll later regret. Wait for the Isaac He has promised for you.

Chapter 15

BURDENS

Check Your Baggage Here

Jesus said, "Come to me, all you who are weary and burdened, and I will give you rest. Take my yoke upon you and learn from me, for I am gentle and humble in heart, and you will find rest for your souls. For my yoke is easy and my burden is light." (Matthew 11:28–30 NIV)

According to legend a Christian who was weary from carrying his cross passed through a small village. He noticed a sign in front of a store that read "Crosses Traded Here." Thinking his load was unfair and his cross too heavy, he decided to enter the store. He was amazed to discover it was filled wall to wall with crosses. He told the owner, "My cross is really heavy, and I'd like to trade it for a different one."

The owner replied, "Very well. You can trade your cross for any one of these crosses carried by the saints throughout the ages. Choose the easiest one."

The man approached a stack of crosses, comparing them for size and comfort. He picked up one, but it was much heavier than his. He picked up the next cross, and it was even heavier than the first. He moved to the next one, then the next, but they were all much heavier than his.

After going through the entire store, he finally came to the last cross and picked it up with ease. "I'll trade my cross for this one," the relieved man told the owner.

"But sir," the owner replied, "that is the cross you carried in here!"

Sometimes we think our burdens are too heavy until we compare them with the persecutions of the saints from the past. Even though our trials are light in comparison, some of the burdens we carry can still be overwhelming. At times almost unbearable. If we don't find a way to deal with them, we will be crushed under the weight.

Some people try to lighten their loads through counseling. One woman was heavily burdened with problems and decided to see a counselor. She explained, "I have so many problems, they're giving me a migraine headache."

The counselor said, "Please sit down and tell me about it."

She sat down and unloaded her problems for three hours. When she had finished, she said, "I feel so much better now. My headache has disappeared."

The counselor replied, "No, it hasn't. I've got it now."

We can't release our burdens without giving them to someone else. Jesus said He wants to take our burdens and give us rest. But if this is true, why do so many Christians still feel weighed down with problems? Surely Jesus wasn't lying when He said we could find rest for our souls.

Perhaps there's another explanation. Maybe the problem lies with our inability to release our burdens.

The Luggage of Life

Burdens are the invisible suitcases we carry through life. We don't transport them with our hands or on our backs. We carry this baggage on our souls. When we feel burdened down, we're not going to see a physical load; that's because it's invisible. Even so, we aren't just imagining this pressure that weighs us down. It's not a physical burden but a spiritual weight that's causing the heaviness on our souls.

We acquire these burdens when we think about problems for prolonged periods. Of course no one is exempt from having problems. But if we keep mulling them over in our minds, they attach themselves to us and keep us from enjoying life.

I once was with a group on a seven-day tour of Israel. On the third day of the tour, I could see that a pastor friend of mine wasn't enjoying the trip because his mind was back in the United States. He had been thinking about some problems in his church and was missing the opportunity of the moment.

Finally I said, "Paul, snap out of it! We've been in Israel for three days, and it's like you're not even here. If you don't quit thinking about your church and start enjoying it here, in a few days we'll be flying back home, and you will have missed the entire trip!"

My pep talk jarred him back to reality, and he enjoyed the final days of the tour because he let go of what was bothering him. And you must do the same.

Accumulating Excess Baggage

The burdens we carry on our souls are produced by difficulties we encounter every day. They may be real or imaginary, but both will affect us in the same way. Even what we perceive to be problems can weigh us down.

Although we may be able to carry some baggage without becoming weary, burdens can accumulate with time. Just as a weight lifter adds weights to his barbell, we can add weights to our souls. Every time we experience a difficult problem, it becomes potential baggage to our load. When another problem comes along, if we don't learn to release it, it too will be added.

As we continue stacking one problem on top of another like layers of a sandwich, we will eventually get depressed. Jesus referred to this state of the soul as being "weary and burdened." That's why Jesus said we will find "rest for your souls" if we will come to Him.

Some time ago a small airplane crashed because too much baggage had been loaded on board. The extra weight kept the plane from climbing to its desired altitude after takeoff, and the plane crashed into some trees. Too much baggage loaded on our souls will not only hinder us from reaching our highest potential, but will also take us down.

Most of us never stop to think how we pick up these extra loads as we travel through life.

A little girl is cruelly teased and rejected by the other students in school. It devastates her, and she starts believing that no one will ever love her. A burden is placed on her soul that she will carry for the next fifteen years.

A young lady makes a vow to stay a virgin until she gets married. But in the backseat of a car, her boyfriend goes too far. She gave in just one time, but she picked up a burden that night. It will continue to haunt her, especially on her wedding night. Until she receives God's forgiveness, her relationship with the Lord and her husband will be adversely affected. A ten-year burden.

A businessman can't get all his work done at the office, so he brings it home. He has no time for his wife or children. Bills need to be paid, so work comes first. He's carrying too many burdens and doesn't even realize it until his wife asks for a divorce. A burden for the rest of his life.

Just because we may have dealt with a problem twenty years ago doesn't mean that it's gone and no longer affects us. We may have packed it away in one of the suitcases that we're carrying through life.

We must all carry some luggage as we travel toward our destination, but we don't need to carry more bags than are necessary. If we are going to have a successful journey, we must check the baggage we are lugging and leave behind the unnecessary ones.

Checking Your Baggage

Let's say you've booked a flight to another city. Before you are permitted to board the plane, you must first have your baggage checked. Airport security is looking for a couple of things. First, they'll put your bag on a scale to make sure it's not overweight. If the limit is fifty pounds per bag, they won't let you take a hundred-pound suitcase with you. Second, they're looking to see if you're carrying anything harmful or dangerous. It's okay for you to carry clothes with you, but not bombs.

Have you ever checked the baggage you're carrying on your soul? You wonder why you're depressed or burning out. It's because you're holding on to heavy burdens that are weighing you down. You might also be carrying explosive attitudes in your luggage, which are causing you to self-destruct. God didn't design you to carry so much excess and harmful baggage, so you've got to let it go.

Jesus said, "Come to me, all you who are weary and burdened, and I will give you rest. Take my yoke upon you and learn from me, for I am gentle and humble in heart, and you will find rest for your souls. For my yoke is easy and my burden is light" (Matthew 11:28–30 NIV).

He said, "Learn from me." We carry too much baggage because we haven't *learned* from Jesus how to properly live. He also said, "My burden is light." The Greek word for "burden" means "a load that you carry." A burden is an invisible but real weight that you carry on your soul.

If you go hiking with a pack on your back, you'll get physically tired and weary after a while. After you've carried a heavy spiritual backpack for a while, your soul will get weary and tired. You'll say things like, "I'm really tired, but I haven't done any work to make me tired." "I'm depressed." "I am stressed out." "I'm burned out." "I've had it!" "I can't take it anymore!"

Sleeping gives you rest for your body, but Jesus is the only one who can give you rest for your soul. To check your baggage, you must open your cases for inspection. We pack our excess baggage in three distinct suitcases—the past, the present, and the future.

Past baggage

The past doesn't exist anymore, except in your memory, and so the only way you can carry baggage from the past is in your mind. Although you can live only in the present, your mind can drift to another "time zone," and it's easy to get stuck there. People carrying past baggage have their minds stuck somewhere back in time.

Everyone is carrying a different set of memories. I'm the only one on the planet who has traveled the exclusive path of my life's journey, so my memories of life's experiences are unique to me. Likewise, you're the only one who has traveled down your path, so your experiences have created your own unique memories. That means only you can inspect your baggage, because you're the only one who knows what's in there.

Your entire life up until right now is in the past. I know you have a lot of memories in that bag, but some of them may be destroying you. Some of your experiences were good, while others were bad. Your good memories are fine, but it's those bad recollections that will turn into excess baggage.

As you travel down Bad Memory Lane, you drag all your regrets from the past as extra luggage. Some people drive down the highway of life with their eyes fixed on the rearview mirror. Their conversations usually revolve around hurts or mistakes that occurred earlier in their lives. They want more than anything to go back in time and change what happened. But because time travel isn't possible, their only two options are to keep venting their frustrations or to find a way to have closure with their past.

People who are stuck in the Past Time Zone are "if only" people. "If only I hadn't made that mistake in the past." "If only I had married Bill instead of Bob, then I'd have a happy marriage." "If only I had not been abused as a child, I wouldn't be bitter." "If only I had chosen a different career, I wouldn't have financial problems."

They keep recalling things that happened ten or twenty years ago, as if those things happened yesterday. Those past incidents have been forgotten by everyone else in the world, but the "if only" person carries the past baggage on his or her soul every day. You can't change your past, but your past can change you—if you don't let go of it.

I was once the guest speaker at a church and preached on forgiving your enemies. A woman came to me after church and said, "I just can't forgive my mother. Every single day I think about all the awful things she did to me growing up."

"What are some of the good things she did for you?" I asked.

"My mother didn't do one good thing for me my entire life."

"She gave birth to you," I replied. "Isn't that one good thing?"

"That's the *only* good thing she did for me."

This woman was clearly bitter, so I said, "Jesus died for you and her. You need to sit down with her and have a heart-to-heart talk. Tell her that you forgive her."

"I can't," she protested. "She's been dead for three years."

This woman carried her dead mother in her suitcase every day. She couldn't let go because her fingers were so tightly gripped to luggage handles. By clinging to past hurts, she chose to keep tormenting herself instead of enjoying her life today.

Future baggage

Future baggage is the luggage we pack for all the trips in the years to come. Worry concerns itself with every bad possibility that might occur in the future. If you're carrying this excess baggage, follow the steps listed in chapter 9, "Worry: The Movies in Your Mind."

Whenever we worry, we envision all the disasters that could happen to us or those we love. We're fearful that God won't provide our future needs. Inside this suitcase, we pack the fear of car wrecks, diseases, misfortunes, and Murphy's Law (if anything can go wrong, it will).

People who are stuck in the Future Time Zone are "what if" people. "What if I lose my job?" "What if terrorists strike?" "What if my house is burglarized?" The list of what-if questions is endless.

In the middle of the night a couple heard a noise in their house. The husband went downstairs to investigate and found a burglar putting their silverware in a bag. He told the burglar, "Wait right here. I want to go get my wife. She's been expecting you every night for the past twenty years!"

Faith is "the assurance of things hoped for" (Hebrews 11:1). Worry is just the opposite. It's the assurance of things *not* hoped for. It's actually negative faith because it believes bad things will come to pass. Even if no disasters have actually occurred, we visualize these calamities in our minds as if they were guaranteed to happen.

Are you afraid whenever you think about the future? If so, it's probably because you're not trusting God to be in control and take care of you. The disciples asked Jesus what were the signs of His Second Coming. He said, "You will be hearing of wars and rumors of wars. See that you are not frightened" (Matthew 24:6). Jesus picked a "worst-case scenario" about wars taking place all over the world, which can be frightening, but He specifically told us to *"see that you are not frightened."*

He couldn't say that unless He has complete control over those future events. Obviously, He has to have control over those events or He couldn't predict them. He also couldn't say it unless He's watching over each one of us. He couldn't tell us to not be afraid unless He would be present to protect and provide for us. Trusting His words will keep us from picking up future baggage.

Present baggage

You can't live in the past, and you can't live the future. The only place you can live is the present, and it's also the only time you can manage your burdens. Present baggage may involve marital difficulties, overdue bills, strained relationships, or problems at work.

You'll get overloaded with present burdens by taking on too many responsibilities. If you are trying to manage an overabundance of activities at one time, your baggage can get too heavy to carry.

Sometimes we pick up other people's luggage and start carrying their burdens along with ours. Although God will lead you to help some people, it's impossible to help everyone. Some people won't take responsibility for themselves, so they'll dump all their problems on you, which can turn into another heavy burden.

What would happen to you if you tried to carry the burdens of every person in your state? You couldn't do it. It would crush you. You can't even carry the burdens of every person in your church. You can help a few people, but God doesn't call you to carry everyone's load.

If you're carrying someone else's baggage and it's wearing you out, then the Lord may be telling you to let go of it. It might be a burden God never called you to carry.

To handle your present baggage, you may need to slow down. Don't be in such a hurry. We're the only country in the world with a mountain named Rushmore. Take your time as you take a closer look at what you're doing. What activity do you need to stop doing because it's wearing you out?

Do you realize that God does not call you to do *everything*? You need to do only those things that He has called you to do. You'll remember that Martha in the Bible was someone who liked to keep busy. When Jesus and His disciples show up unexpectedly at her house, Martha welcomes them in, but she immediately starts trying to figure out how she's going to feed them all.

She's thinking, *Okay, thirteen men, so that's four meatloaves and three apple pies.* She's in the kitchen pulling out the pots and pans, looking through her recipe box. As she runs around the kitchen gathering ingredients, she gets increasingly stressed out. Martha is miffed that her sister, Mary, won't get up and help her.

Martha starts loudly clanging pots and clearing her throat, hoping that Mary will somehow get the message. She doesn't. Mary's too captivated by what Jesus is saying. Mary is nodding her head as she listens to Him teach, carefully taking notes. God in a human body is sitting in her living room, revealing the truths of His kingdom, but Martha is trying to figure out if the meatloaf needs more salt.

Finally Martha can't take it anymore. She stomps into the living room and interrupts the Bible study. With hands on her hips, she commands Jesus to straighten out her sister. "Lord, do You not care that my sister has left me to do all the serving alone? Then tell her to help me" (Luke 10:40).

Of course Martha is expecting to hear Jesus reply, "Martha, you're so right. Doesn't anyone here remember my teachings on being a servant? Take a look at my servant, Martha. So humble. So dedicated. Mary, you could learn a few things from her. So get up and go help her set the table for dinner."

Instead, Jesus says something no one was expecting. "Martha, Martha, you are worried and bothered about so many things; but only one thing is necessary, for Mary has chosen the good part, which shall not be taken away from her" (Luke 10:41–42).

He said Martha was "worried and bothered." It's a good question to ask everyone. What are you worried about? What are you bothered about? Whatever it is, that's baggage you don't need to be carrying.

Martha was worried and bothered "about *so many* things." In other words, Jesus is saying, "Martha, you're carrying too much baggage. You're doing things that I didn't call you to do, and that's why you're worried, and that's why you're bothered."

Jesus continued, "But only *one thing* is necessary, and Mary has chosen it." If only one thing is necessary, that means Martha was carrying "unnecessary baggage." What she was doing wasn't wrong, but her priorities were. Most of us also carry unnecessary suitcases, because our priorities are in the wrong order.

You never know, but maybe if Martha had sat with Mary and listened, Jesus might have said, "Martha, if you will just pull out your leftovers, I will multiply them for you." If we will do what is needful, He will take care of the other things.

Now imagine carrying the past, future, and present baggage on top of your soul. Can you feel the pressure? That's a lot of baggage! It's time to let go and leave them behind.

Don't Claim Your Baggage

Just because you've carried your luggage this far doesn't mean you have to keep carrying it. Leave it at the baggage claim by doing two things.

1. *Let go of all excess baggage.*

We can let go of our excess baggage only by giving it to the Lord. Because He cares for us, He is concerned about every one of our problems. However, God does not automatically remove our excess baggage from us. By a deliberate act of our own will, we must cast our burdens on Him. "Casting all your care upon him; for he careth for you" (1 Peter 5:7 KJV).

Whenever we cast something, we throw it in a certain direction. Two people are playing catch; one person lets go of the ball and hurls it into the hands of the other person. When we cast our burdens to the Lord, we release them out of our hands and place them in His hands. Then we will no longer regret the past, be depressed by the present, or worry about the future. All our burdens are now in God's hands.

But we can easily fool ourselves into thinking we've let go of our problems when we really haven't. We might cast them to the Lord with a string attached and then pull them back, like a yo-yo. Although we make an attempt to release them, we never really do. We've got to permanently let go if we want to be free.

BURDENS

A little boy got his hand stuck in an expensive vase. His parents tried everything to get his hand out. They tried soap and grease, but nothing worked. They finally decided they had no other choice but to break it.

His father got out a hammer and was ready to shatter the vase. Just before he hit it, he stopped and asked, "Jimmy, are you holding on to anything?"

"Yes, Daddy," he answered.

"What are you holding on to?"

"I'm holding on to a nickel."

"Let go of the nickel, Jimmy," his father commanded.

"But I don't want to."

"Son, you have to let go if you want to be set free."

The boy let go of the coin, and his hand easily slipped out.

Many people hold on to their excess baggage, refusing to let go. But if they would simply release whatever they are holding on to, they would be free from the things keeping them in spiritual bondage.

One woman in my church was repeatedly struck by tragedy. Her young daughter was diagnosed with diabetes; her young son was diagnosed with juvenile rheumatoid arthritis; her mother-in-law had a heart attack; her own mother died suddenly; and her house caught on fire—all within a seven-week period. Her burdens brought her to the verge of a breakdown.

She realized if she didn't find a way to let go of the excess baggage, she would collapse under the pressure. She decided to write down on a piece of paper twenty-five burdens she was carrying, along with a prayer to God. Then she put them inside five balloons, filled them with helium, and released them to the Lord.

She watched the balloons float away until they were out of her sight. As they disappeared she felt a tremendous release in her spirit. The invisible weights lifted off her soul, because she symbolically cast her burdens to the Lord and let them go. Just as you can feel a physical weight lifted from your body, you can also sense when a spiritual burden is released from your soul.

Joe was walking to the Laundromat, carrying over his shoulder a duffel bag stuffed with dirty clothes. On the way he met his friend

Darlene, who had been weighed down with a number of problems. Joe reminded her that she needed to cast her burdens to the Lord instead of carrying them herself.

Darlene said, "I thought I gave them to the Lord, but I still feel burdened. How will I know if I have released them?"

Joe let go of the sack, and the laundry bag fell off his back to the ground. "How do I know that I dropped the sack? I haven't looked around to see if it's off my back."

"You know because it's not weighing you down anymore."

"And that's how you'll know if you've released your burdens to the Lord. You will feel the weight lifted off your soul."

2. *Carry only enough baggage for today's journey.*

It would be crazy to pack suitcases for future trips. Any luggage you don't need for today's journey is excess baggage. Jesus said, "So don't be anxious about tomorrow. God will take care of your tomorrow too. Live one day at a time" (Matthew 6:34 TLB). Living one day at a time will keep you from carrying too many burdens.

You can't go back in time and relive your past. Although you can't unscramble eggs, you can make an omelet out of them. You also can't go forward in time and live in the future. Most of the things you worry about will never happen. Although you don't know what the future holds, you do know who holds the future. Trusting God to take care of your future will keep you from handling that extra luggage. You can *learn* from the past, and *look* to the future, but you can only *live* in the present.

A clock thought about how often it would have to tick during the coming year. Figuring two ticks a second, 120 a minute, 7,200 each hour, 172,800 a day, and 1,209,600 ticks every week, the clock realized it would have to tick nearly 63 million times in the next year. The more it thought about this, the worse it felt. Finally, the clock had a nervous breakdown.

It went to the clock psychiatrist and said, "I can't go on. I don't know how I'll ever make it through the next year."

The doctor responded, "How many ticks can you tick at a time?"

"Only one."

"Well, if you will tick one tick at a time and not worry about the next tick, you'll be just fine."

So the clock followed his advice and ticked through the next year, then the next, and the next. . . . And, as all good stories end, it ticked happily ever after.

Just as a clock can tick only one tick at a time, you can live only one day at a time. If you'll learn to take each day as it comes, without dragging up the past or grasping for the future, life will become amazingly easy.

Once God has lifted your burdens, don't even think about reclaiming your excess baggage. Keep your hands off those suitcase handles, and your journey will be a lot more enjoyable.

Chapter 16

DEPRESSION

Singing in the Dark

Then Jezebel sent a messenger to Elijah, saying, "So may the gods
do to me and even more, if I do not make your life as the life of
one of them by tomorrow about this time." And he was afraid and
arose and ran for his life. . . . But he himself went a day's journey
into the wilderness, and came and sat down under a juniper tree;
and he requested for himself that he might die, and said, "It is
enough; now, O LORD, take my life." (1 Kings 19:2–4)

God's prophet Elijah challenged the 850 prophets of Baal and Asherah
on Mount Carmel and prayed for fire to come down from heaven. God
sent down fire and consumed the sacrifice. Then Elijah went down to
the brook Kishon and slew the false prophets.

What an act of faith! What an example of courage!

King Ahab rode back to Jezreel to report the news to his wife, Jezebel. You can just imagine evil Jezebel eagerly waiting for her husband
to return. When she saw his chariot returning from Mount Carmel, she
assumed he had good news. But when Ahab walked into their palace,
she could read defeat all over his face. She asked, "What happened to
the prophets of Baal?"

"They're all dead," Ahab answered. "Elijah had them killed."

Jezebel was furious. You'd think she would be terrified of a man like this, but not so. Instead, she sent a text message to Elijah: "U R dead by 2morrow. —Jez."

When Elijah read the message, butterflies started fluttering in his stomach. His knees grew weak and wobbly. He lost his courage and ran for his life.

What an act of unbelief! What an example of cowardice!

How could he go from feeling so high to so low in so short a period? Just hours before this, he had celebrated a victorious contest on Mount Carmel. Now he was hiding in shame and depressed in the wilderness.

Elijah forgot about all the miracles God had done through him. He failed to remember when God multiplied the widow's oil and flour, and raised her son from the dead. He forgot about the rain-stopping miracle and calling down fire from heaven. Depression makes us forget about God's power because it leaves Him out of the picture.

When we're depressed, we lose all awareness of God's presence, protection, and provision. This dark cloud surrounds us so that we can't see anything worth living for. We feel totally abandoned by friends and loved ones. Life loses its meaning. Elijah was at such a low point he wanted to die.

Signs of Depression

How did he lose his perspective? Can it happen to us? Here are three signs that you are slipping into depression.

Sign 1: *Your situation looks undefeatable.*

At this point in Elijah's life, Jezebel looked more powerful than God. He took his eyes off God and focused on his problem, which blew it out of proportion. Elijah viewed Jezebel through a magnifying glass, and she looked like a scene from the movie *The Attack of the Fifty-Foot Woman*.

During the Civil War, General Robert E. Lee had a shortage of soldiers. His army would be easily defeated if the Union army discovered this weakness. Since he couldn't increase the number of soldiers, he decided he could make his army look larger than it actually was.

He loaded his troops on trains and transported them to different places. At every train station, the same Confederate soldiers were unloaded from the trains. It looked as if thousands of new troops were being transported in and added to the Rebel army.

The Union spies became discouraged, thinking the South had a much larger army than it actually had. General Lee hadn't made his army any larger or more powerful. He was using a psychological tactic to make them look undefeatable. And it worked.

Years ago I counseled a depressed woman who couldn't see anything good happening in her life. In reality, her situation wasn't nearly as bad as she perceived it to be. She had good health and all of her family's needs were met. She had a good job and lived in a nice house in a safe neighborhood. But her outlook on life was so warped that she could only see huge problems. Rather than seeing a big Jesus and a little devil, she saw a big devil and a little Jesus. People can view a glass of water that is half filled differently. Positive people see it as half full. Negative people view it as half empty. This woman saw it as totally empty.

When I counsel people like this, I try to get them to change their outlooks so they will view life in a different way. Changing one's perspective from negative to positive doesn't happen overnight. It's a gradual process that takes place day by day through the renewing of one's mind (see Romans 12:2). But this woman wanted a quick solution with no effort on her part, so she quit coming to counseling.

If you are under the cloud of depression, you must choose to change the way you view your circumstances. You must look at the big picture, not just the one or two things that are pulling you down. Rather than complaining about your problems, start thanking God for your blessings. View the glass as half full not half empty. See a big Jesus and a little devil.

The only one who can change your thought patterns is you. Your situation is not as bad as it seems, so quit magnifying it in your mind.

Sign 2: *You are consumed with thoughts about yourself.*

In his depression Elijah told God, "I alone am left; and they seek my life, to take it away" (1 Kings 19:10). Depression makes us think only about ourselves and makes us say, "No one cares about me." "Why hasn't anyone visited me?" "No one has bigger problems than I have."

Elijah felt abandoned and thought he was the only one in his predicament. The apostle Peter wrote to a group of Christians who thought they were the only ones who were experiencing trials. He told them to resist Satan, "knowing that the same experiences of suffering are being accomplished by your brethren who are in the world" (1 Peter 5:9). He told them that because it helps to know that, when trials come, we are not alone.

When Elijah thought he was the only one left, God told him, "Yet I will leave 7,000 in Israel, all the knees that have not bowed to Baal and every mouth that has not kissed him" (1 Kings 19:18). Not only was God aware of what Elijah was going through, but He also knew exactly how many others were going through the same experiences. God was aware of their problems back then, and He is also aware of the struggles you are experiencing right now.

Sign 3: *You've lost hope for the future.*

In his depression Elijah requested that "he might die" (1 Kings 19:4). He was fleeing from being killed, yet he prayed to die. Sometimes our prayers don't make much sense when we're depressed. Elijah was bewildered in the wilderness. He lost hope for the future and had given up.

The irony of the situation was that Elijah prayed for death, yet he never died. He was caught up alive in a whirlwind to heaven without tasting death (2 Kings 2:11). Little did he realize during his time of depression that God had great plans for him. Depression will always blind us of hope for the future.

Something to Think About

Do you understand why you get depressed? I'd like to give you a little test to help you analyze yourself.

The Thought-Analyzer Test

1. When I am happy, I have been thinking _____ thoughts.

2. When I am sad, I have been thinking _____ thoughts.

3. When I am angry, I have been thinking _____ thoughts.

4. When I am depressed, I have been thinking _____ thoughts.

The answers are:

1. happy
2. sad
3. angry
4. depressing

It is so profoundly simple that it is simply profound. The way we think affects the moods we are in. Thoughts do affect emotions. My thoughts tell my emotions what to do. Emotions respond to the information that is fed to them.

For example, if I go to a horror movie, I experience fear even though I know what I am watching is not real. If I watch a sad movie, I may cry because my emotions have been touched by my thoughts. A comedy can put me in a jovial mood. Thoughts have a powerful effect upon emotions.

If I have been depressed, it is because I have been thinking depressing thoughts. Although some depression is caused by poor diet and lack of exercise, the vast majority of cases are caused because people have been dwelling upon depressing thoughts. I cannot keep thinking negative thoughts without becoming depressed.

That is the problem. But it is also the solution to the problem. If my thoughts determine my emotions, then my depression can be reversed by changing the way I think.

Feelings follow thoughts like a caboose lags behind a locomotive. If my "thought locomotive" goes into the valley, then my "feelings caboose" will follow it down into the valley. But if the locomotive goes up a mountain, although the caboose lags behind the train at first, it will eventually follow it up the mountain.

If I want my emotions to be turned around, I must reverse the way I think. Rather than thinking depressing thoughts, I choose to think joyful thoughts. At first I may not feel like rejoicing, but if I will keep thinking joyful thoughts, eventually I will become joyful.

Thinking positively releases chemicals called endorphins into our bodies that correct the chemical imbalances caused by depression. Although God didn't explain to us the medical reasons for rejoicing, he did tell us that "a joyful heart is good medicine" (Proverbs 17:22).

A cartoon depicted a skinny man with long hair and a long beard, hanging by chains on the wall of a dungeon. He had obviously been hanging there a long time. A psychiatrist sat in a chair in front of him, taking notes as he listened to the man. The man hanging on the wall, grinning from ear to ear, said, "Call me weird, but I feel good!"

Yes, it is possible to feel good in spite of your gloomy circumstances. You can see whatever you want in your situation. Two young boys were raised in the home of an alcoholic father. As young men, each went his own way. Years later a psychologist, who was analyzing the effects of alcoholism on children, searched out these two men.

One had turned out to be like his alcoholic father. The counselor asked him, "Why did you become an alcoholic?"

The son answered, "What else would you expect if you had a father like mine?"

When the psychologist found the other son, he was amazed to discover he had never taken a drink in his life. He asked, "Why did you decide to never drink alcohol?"

The other son answered, "What else would you expect if you had a father like mine?"[1]

The two boys grew up under the same circumstances and turned out completely different. Why? Because it is not what you go through that determines what you will become. It's how you respond that determines what you will become.

The first son claimed to be a victim of his circumstances. The second son used his horrible upbringing as a motivation to stay away from alcohol. Same circumstances, different responses. Everyone is either a victim or a victor. Which are you? You get to choose.

Conquering the Depression Giant

Although depression makes you believe that it's impossible to get out of it, you must understand the freedom is indeed possible. Crack open the door of hope and allow the light to come through. You have to believe that freedom is possible before you can apply any of these suggestions to your life. Here are several positive steps you can take to conquer depression.

1. *Pray for your depression to leave.*

Perhaps you're saying, "Pray for it to go away? That sounds too simple." Sometimes the simple solutions are the right ones. Naaman in the Old Testament was cured of his leprosy by doing something easy (see 2 Kings 5:9–14). It doesn't have to be complicated.

God can do anything, including removing your depression. Jeremiah 32:27 says, "Behold, I am the LORD, the God of all flesh; is anything too difficult for Me?" Jesus added, "The things that are impossible with people are possible with God" (Luke 18:27). With God's supernatural help, it's possible for your depression to leave.

I know a woman who was in deep depression. Some women in her church offered to pray for her. After they laid their hands on her and prayed for the depression to leave, this woman said, "I felt something like electricity coming into me." Instantly her depression lifted and her countenance changed. It has never come back, even after several years have passed. Her healing came as a direct answer to prayer.

In Mark 5:25–34, a woman had a hemorrhage for twelve years but hadn't been cured, even after being treated by many physicians. One day as Jesus passed through her town, the crowd was pressing in on Him. This woman came up behind Him and touched His garment. Immediately power proceeded out of Him and went into her. The blood instantly dried up and "she *felt in her body* that she was healed" (v. 29).

When I have interviewed people who have been healed through prayer, some have felt God's power coming into them, while others felt nothing at all. Don't depend on your feelings; you can still be healed without feeling anything.

On another occasion a woman visited the church where I was preaching. During my sermon I mentioned that God had the power to set people free from depression. At the end of the service, she came forward and asked for prayer, saying that she was deeply depressed. When the prayer team prayed for her, her depression instantly left.

Afterward she said, "I was so deeply depressed that I thought about killing myself this week, but thoughts kept coming into my mind telling me to come visit this church. Now I know why. God led me here to set me free from my depression!"

Later I contacted this woman and asked if her depression was still gone. She said, "Yes, it left me that day when they prayed for me. I feel completely different now because I'm free!"

Jesus came "to proclaim release to the captives" and "to set free those who are oppressed" (Luke 4:18). That certainly includes those who are depressed. Here is a suggested prayer of freedom: "Lord, I ask You to have mercy on me. Please set me free from this depression so I can joyfully serve You. I command this depression to leave me now, in Jesus' name."

2. *Think positively instead of negatively.*

Dr. Michael Jacobson cited a study in which patients were asked to recall various types of emotional experiences while doctors monitored how it affected their bodies. All the patients were asked to relive the experience in their minds for five minutes.

When the patients thought for five minutes about situations that made them angry or frustrated, their antibody levels dropped 55 percent. Six hours later their immune system was still depressed. Conversely, when the patients relived situations that were meaningful and made them happy, their antibody levels rose 40 percent and stayed elevated six hours later.[2] This study reveals that your body is affected either positively or negatively by the way you think.

As we've already stated, the way you think will determine how you feel. Change your thoughts, and you'll change your feelings. Someone has said, "What you *tune* into is what you *turn* into." Deprogram your mind from negative thinking and reprogram it with uplifting thoughts.

The apostle Paul said, "Finally, brethren, whatever is true, whatever is honorable, whatever is right, whatever is pure, whatever is lovely, whatever is of good repute, if there is any excellence and if anything worthy of praise, dwell on these things" (Philippians 4:8). Read it again, and you'll see that depressing thoughts aren't on that list.

Years ago a friend of mine struggled with depression and thoughts of taking his life. He described it as a "house of depressing thoughts inside my mind" that he lived in. He would leave "the house" for short periods of time and would feel better, but then he kept going back to it and his depression would return.

When he gave his life to Jesus, the Lord showed him a picture in his mind of the house of depressing thoughts being destroyed. He realized he could never go back to that place in his thought life. Since that day, whenever a thought came that would lead to depression, he would say, "I left that house of depressing and suicidal thoughts on the day Jesus destroyed it. It doesn't exist anymore, so I can't return there." By replacing his negative thoughts with positive ones, his depression has never returned. He is now serving the Lord as a missionary.

3. *Express your positive thoughts by verbalizing them.*

What you say has a profound influence on the way you feel. As you've started thinking positively, you must now *verbalize* what you've being thinking, through thanksgiving, rejoicing, and praising. These three expressions are powerful weapons for fighting off depression. Thanksgiving is speaking your appreciation for what He has done. Rejoicing is expressing joyfulness regardless of the circumstances. Praising is exalting God for who He is.

Thanksgiving

Continually thanking God for His goodness is one of the most powerful things you can do to demolish depressing thoughts. Being genuinely thankful will not only drive away depressing thoughts, but will also bring you joy. Thankfulness and joy are linked together. "In everything give thanks; for this is God's will for you in Christ Jesus" (1 Thessalonians 5:18).

Novelist A. J. Cronin tells of a physician friend who often prescribed a "thank-you" cure for depressed people. For six weeks the patient needed to say "thank you" for every kindness and keep a record of it. According to Cronin, the doctor had a remarkable cure rate.

Try it and you'll see. Thanking God for all things will change your attitude.

Rejoicing

Where does joy come from? Jesus promised to put His joy inside every believer. He said, "These things I have spoken to you so that My joy may be in you, and that your joy may be made full" (John 15:11). Notice that our joy is linked to His joy.

Rejoicing is the act of verbally expressing your joy. We are to "rejoice in the Lord always" (Philippians 4:4). "Always" means at all times, even when you are feeling down and blue. Telling a depressed person to rejoice is like asking a man with broken legs to dance. You may not feel like doing it, but do it anyway and you'll find that joy will fill your heart.

Praising

Praising God has tremendous power to displace depression. God tells us to put on "the garment of praise for the spirit of heaviness" (Isaiah 61:3 KJV). The spirit of heaviness means depression. Praising can also involve singing to the Lord.

When the Moabites and Ammonites were about to attack Jerusalem, King Jehoshaphat did something to defend the city that looked totally insane. He gathered those who sang to the Lord and praised Him in the temple and dressed them in holy attire. Then he sent them ahead of the army into the battle (2 Chronicles 20:21–22). Why would he send out people to sing and praise God first—and put the soldiers behind them? It's because God wants us to sing and praise *before* we see the victory. Praise is a statement of faith that the Lord will win the battle. And that's exactly what happened. God defeated the enemies, and Israel didn't even have to fight. It's amazing what praising can do!

God wants you to sing and praise Him as you battle the giant of depression. David said, "The LORD will command His lovingkindness in the daytime; / And His song will be with me in the night" (Psalm 42:8). If you are going through a dark time, sing in the dark. Listen to praise music and sing along with it. Continue singing to the Lord until your depression leaves.

Some of the most beautiful singing canaries in the world have come from the Harz Mountains of Germany. During World War I, it became impossible to obtain these little warblers. A dealer in New York came up with the idea of training an American finch to sing like the European variety. He asked for the songs of the German birds to be recorded and mailed to his home. When they arrived, he kept playing them over and over in the room where he kept his own canaries.

At first his idea of training his birds to sing met with little success. Then one day he made a startling discovery. He found that if he covered their cages and completely shut out the light, his American birds soon learned to sing like the birds on the recording. They learned to sing in the dark.[3]

You also must learn to sing during life's dark times. You might not see what lies ahead because your vision is restricted by the darkness of despair. But that's the best time to sing. It will help you endure the dark times until the morning light arrives.

4. *Put your hope in God.*

David, who wrote many of the psalms, had times when even he battled with despair. He gave us the answer when he wrote,

> Why are you in despair, O my soul?
> And why have you become disturbed within me?
> Hope in God. (Psalm 42:5)

If you have lost all hope, you will find it if you will look to God.

Everyone needs something good to look forward to. David wrote, "I would have despaired unless I had believed that I would see the goodness of the LORD / In the land of the living" (Psalm 27:13). Depression takes away your hope so that you have nothing to look forward to. To drive away your depression, you must begin to hope again. You might not have hope in your circumstances, but you can always have hope in God because He has a good future planned for you.

You will find hope as you draw closer to God. "Draw near to God and He will draw near to you" (James 4:8). Nearness isn't talking about your distance from God but your intimacy with Him. A man and wife can be standing side by side, yet be far away from each other in their hearts. Draw closer to God in your heart by seeking what He wants for you.

A man in a rowboat was caught in a current and was floating downstream toward a waterfall. As he was drifting away, he saw a large rock on the riverbank. The rock provided security and stability for the man who was about to lose hope. He threw a rope around the rock and pulled the boat toward it. As he drew near to the rock, the rock drew near to him.

When we call out to God for help, we are throwing out the rope to the Rock. "To You, O LORD, I call; My Rock" (Psalm 28:1). As we draw near to God's throne of grace, the Lord will draw near to us. The throne of grace is where we'll "find grace to help in time of need" (Hebrews 4:16).

5. *Reach out and help others.*

Instead of saying, "Nobody loves me," say, "How can I help someone?" Booker T. Washington said, "If you want to lift yourself up, lift up someone else." By turning your eyes outwardly, it keeps you from focusing inwardly, which feeds depression. God tells us, "Do not merely look out for your own personal interests, but also for the interests of others" (Philippians 2:4). You cannot sow love and reap depression.

Dr. Viktor Frankl, an Austrian physician, was imprisoned in one of Hitler's death camps. He and his fellow Jewish people suffered unbelievable atrocities. Over a period of time, he made an insightful discovery. In his book *Man's Search for Meaning,* he said those people who kept their strength and sanity the longest were those who helped other prisoners and shared what little they had. Their physical and mental condition seemed to be strengthened by their friendliness, compassion, and focus on something other than themselves.[4]

Depressed people are consumed with thoughts about themselves. This inward thinking causes a person to sink even deeper into depression. The way out is to turn your eyes from inward to outward. Instead of feeling sorry for yourself, reach out to other people and meet their needs. If you will do this, you will find that your depression will go away.

6. Determine in your heart that you'll defeat your giant.

Everyone in Israel, except for young David, was afraid to fight Goliath the giant. David told King Saul, "Let no man's heart fail on account of him; your servant will go and fight with this Philistine" (1 Samuel 17:32). He had determined in his heart that he would defeat Goliath.

A number of years ago my mother-in-law sank into deep depression. Her mother had been deeply depressed and eventually committed suicide. Now Barbara was afraid the same thing might happen to her, but she kept her feelings of despair to herself. Week after week, her depression got worse and wouldn't leave. She realized this wasn't the kind of depression most people experience but had reached the point of being a serious problem. The weeks turned into months, and she was losing all hope of being cured.

During this time Barbara and her husband, Neil, drove from Texas to Kansas to visit us. As she watched the miles go by, the weight of her deep depression caused her to sink even lower. She had always trusted the Lord but for some reason had not handed this problem over to Him. At that point, she prayed, "Lord, I don't think I can get out of this on my own. You will have to do it. Please help me."

The next Sunday morning they visited our church before returning home. I preached a message on David and Goliath, "Killing the Giants in Your Life," which is the theme of this book. During the sermon I told the congregation, "Just as God gave David the ability to defeat the giant, He can give you victory over the giant in your life."

Those words challenged Barbara to make a decision to defeat the giant of depression that had been attacking her. In her mind she pictured herself killing the depression. By the end of the message, she realized the heavy weight on her soul had lifted. She felt free for the first time in months.

At first she was hesitant to tell anyone, thinking it might come back. But it has been more than fifteen years now, and the giant of depression is still in the grave. Barbara was set free from her depression because she discovered that God's power was greater than her problem.

Yes, you can be set free from your depression. With God on your side and faith in your heart, the giant of despair will die.

Chapter 17

The Possession Obsession

Do not let your heart envy sinners,
But live in the fear of the LORD always. (Proverbs 23:17)

Are you bothered because your neighbor drives a nicer car than you? Do you crave things that others have? Perhaps you get upset when you work hard while your fellow employees goof off. If so, it sounds like you have a serious case of envy.

I received the following e-mail from a church member who works at a lumberyard:

Dear Pastor Kent,

One of my coworkers is extremely lazy and refuses to do any physical labor. I have always worked my hardest and have been able to keep his laziness from getting to me until today. This afternoon, while I was carrying sheetrock into a house, this lazy guy showed up at the job site. Instead of carrying the sheetrock into the house himself, he made his helper do the work. This made me so mad! Here I was, struggling to do my work, and he was just sitting on his can. I lost my cool, calling him a lazy jerk. I asked if he was going to let the kid do all his work for him. Was I wrong for reacting in this way?

Chris

Here's my reply.

Dear Chris,

Your employer is paying you to do your work, not evaluate his. You aren't just serving your employer but also the Lord (see Colossians 3:23). I know that it's tempting to get mad at lazy workers, but that's not what you are getting paid for. Take your eyes off your coworker and get them back on what God has called you to do.

Pastor Kent

Chris's conflict with his coworker reminds me of the parable Jesus told about a landowner who hired different groups of people to work in his vineyard. The first group agreed to labor all day for a denarius—the wage for a day's work. The last group of laborers worked for only one hour.

At the end of the day the owner paid all his hired men a denarius. The hired hands who worked only one hour were paid the same wage as those who labored twelve hours. The boss's decision to pay everyone alike aggravated the men who had worked all day. Not only did they gripe about their wages, but thought they deserved considerably more pay because they had worked twelve times as long. Note the owner's reaction:

"Friend, I am doing you no wrong; did you not agree with me for a denarius? Take what is yours and go, but I wish to give to this last man the same as to you. Is it not lawful for me to do what I wish with what is my own? Or is your eye envious because I am generous?" (Matthew 20:13–15)

The first group of workers glared with envy at their fellow employees, comparing wages. Have you ever compared your income with someone else's wages, thinking you deserved more?

Analyzing Envy

Sometimes we don't realize that we are viewing others through envy lenses. Envy causes us to compare first, then to covet, and finally to complain. Let's analyze these three steps.

Step 1: *Envy compares.*

Years ago in Manchester, England, a factory worker was responsible for the whistle that marked the beginning and end of the workday. His job was to make sure the clock was accurate. Every day on his way to work, he stopped by a clock shop and set his watch by an expensive clock displayed in the window. Then he set the factory whistle according to the time on his watch.

The owner of the clock shop noticed him stopping by the window every day and asked him what he was doing. The worker explained he set the factory clock by the clock in the window so the factory whistle would blow on time.

The owner laughed. "And to think, all this time I've been setting my clock by your factory whistle."[1]

Many people determine their self-worth by measuring themselves with others. Envy compares incomes, property, and abilities with those who appear to be more prosperous.

Salary envy: "Charlie gets paid twice as much as I do, and he does half the amount of work."

Mansion envy: "Why can't I have a house like the Millers'?"

Talent envy: "I can sing better than she can, so give me the microphone."

Envy compares our clothes and our cars, our jobs and our junk. It bothers us when we see others with something better. Something happens to us when we start comparing. We feel inadequate and inferior. We get upset with those who have it better. The psalmist Asaph said, "For I envied the arrogant when I saw the prosperity of the wicked"

(Psalm 73:3 NIV). We become obsessed with what others possess instead of being thankful for what we have.

A professional basketball player was making millions of dollars, but he was upset because other players on his team were making more. Most people would be thrilled to have his enormous income. But this athlete wasn't happy with his millions. Why? He compared his salary with a few people who made more—not with the multitudes of workers who made significantly less.

I've noticed people always envy those who are more fortunate and never those who are less fortunate. It's easy to get bent out of shape when we start comparing dollars per hour.

A number of years ago, I was talking with a friend who mentioned how much money his brother made, which was a lot. It didn't take me long to calculate that his brother was making four times as much as my salary. Immediately something rose up inside me that made me angry at his brother. And I didn't even know the guy!

In case you haven't figured it out, that "something" that rose up in me was envy. I thought, *That's not right for him to make that much. I'll bet that his job is really easy, too. I wonder what it's like to have that much money. If I had his salary, I could drive a new car instead of the clunker I'm driving now.*

As those devilish thoughts were running through my mind, God interrupted them and said, "What's the matter? Don't you trust Me to provide for you?"

Suddenly I realized that how much money the other guy made wasn't the issue. Why should I ever envy someone if I was truly trusting God to provide for me? If I'm trusting the Lord to meet all my needs, how much money someone else makes shouldn't matter. I was perfectly happy before my friend told me about his salary. But then when I gained that information, my mind went into the "no trespassing" area.

Of course whenever we envy those who are wealthy, we forget about all the work they had to do to get that job. My friend's brother had earned his bachelor's degree, his master's degree, and his doctorate. His education took him years of study, and he probably had to borrow more than $100,000 to pay for his education. But when we're envious, we never think about the huge price they had to pay to get their jobs. As a rule of thumb, the higher paying the job, the more stressful, time-consuming, and demanding it is. But do we think about that? No. Envy just looks at the pay stub.

Step 2: *Envy covets.*

First we make comparisons. Next we start coveting what the other person has. Someone once said the world consists of three kinds of people: The "haves," the "have-nots," and the "have-not-paid-for-what-they-haves." I'd like to add a fourth group: The "have-to-have-what the-'haves'-have." Coveting means that I want something that isn't rightfully mine. The apostle Paul struggled with coveting. "I would not have known about coveting if the Law had not said, 'You shall not covet.' But sin, taking opportunity through the commandment, produced in me coveting of every kind" (Romans 7:7–8).

When I was in sixth grade, I went to a small Lutheran school. Our school didn't have a cafeteria, so each student brought lunch from home and ate it at his or her desk. Every day I carried the same meal in my blue, snap-down lunch box:

Baloney sandwich on white bread (this was before whole wheat bread was "invented")

Small bag of potato chips

Thermos bottle of tomato soup

Moon pie

Robbie Buckner sat to my right. He never brought a lunch box to school. At noon each day, his mother delivered him a hamburger from the restaurant down the street. I came from a low-income family, so I got to eat a hamburger at a restaurant only a couple of times a year. Robbie ate one every day.

Each lunch period I was forced to smell his hamburger. I watched in agony as Robbie opened his mouth wide and bit off a mouthful. It tortured me to listen to him smack each bite, while I forced a baloney sandwich down my own throat.

Paul said, "I would not have known about coveting if the Law had not said, 'You shall not covet.'" I would not have known about coveting if it weren't for Robbie Buckner's hamburger.

I memorized the Ten Commandments in this Christian grade school. I could say the tenth by heart: "You shall not covet your neighbor's house; you shall not covet your neighbor's wife or his male servant or his female servant or his ox or his donkey or anything that belongs to your neighbor" (Exodus 20:17).

With my head I learned *not* to covet, but with my heart I learned *how* to covet. I drooled over my neighbor's hamburger every day at lunchtime. I didn't understand how easily envy could take control of my heart. I started by coveting hamburgers, and later it grew into coveting houses.

I know that hamburgers aren't mentioned in the off-limits list in the tenth commandment. I didn't covet my neighbor's house, wife, servants, ox, or donkey. But that last phrase did me in: "or anything that belongs to your neighbor." Yep, that includes hamburgers.

And who is my neighbor? Everyone except me.

Maybe your problem isn't your neighbor's sandwich, but could it be your neighbor's spouse? Adultery begins through coveting. Stealing starts with coveting. Discontentment is born by coveting. And the list goes on. When coveting consumes one's heart, ungodly actions are soon to follow. "For from within, out of the heart of men, proceed the evil thoughts, fornications, thefts, murders, adulteries, *deeds of coveting* and wickedness, as well as deceit, sensuality, *envy*, slander, pride and foolishness" (Mark 7:21–22).

Step 3: *Envy complains.*

Envy always gets upset when others are blessed. In Jesus' parable when the first group of workers got paid, "they grumbled at the landowner" (Matthew 20:11). The one-hour laborers were paid the same as the all-day workers, which looked like a horrible injustice when viewed through envy glasses.

How did the workers respond to his kindness? They complained to the landowner instead of thanking him for hiring them. They thought he didn't know what he was doing. They forgot that twelve hours earlier they had agreed to work for one denarius, and the landowner paid them that amount. Their employer wasn't being unfair to the all-day laborers; he was simply being generous to the one-hour workers.

If you have a job, didn't you agree to work for a certain amount? If so, then it shouldn't matter what a fellow employee gets paid. If your coworker gets a raise or promotion, it has nothing to do with the agreement you made. If you complain when someone else gets blessed, it's because you're envious. Are you guilty of salary envy?

It's easier to complain about what you don't have than to be thankful for what you do have. Envy always drains thankfulness from your heart.

Exterminating Envy

Some people never realize that envy is the source of their strife with others. James writes, "What is the source of quarrels and conflicts among you? . . . You are envious and cannot obtain, so you fight and quarrel" (James 4:1–2). The source of their quarrels wasn't anger but envy. You can exterminate the giant of envy by doing three things.

1. *Love your neighbor, not what your neighbor has.*

A wealthy elderly man married a beautiful young woman. Not long afterward, he began to wonder if she married him for his money or love for him. He decided to consult with a counselor.

"Doc, my problem is driving me crazy. I need to know if my wife really loves me, or if she just married me for my money."

"The answer is simple," the counselor explained. "Give away all your money, except just enough to live on. If she stays, she loves you. If she leaves, she loves your money."

Envy means you love your neighbor's possessions more than you love your neighbor. Which concerns you the most—your neighbors' material prosperity or their spiritual welfare?

The tenth commandment is the most ignored commandment of them all. Everyone knows thou shall not murder, steal, and commit adultery, because those actions are so destructive. However, the tenth commandment doesn't prohibit an action but goes straight to an attitude in your heart. God says you are not to even *want* what your neighbor has. Coveting is the mastermind inside your heart that draws up the plans on how to carry out the sins of stealing and adultery—not to mention overindulgence. They all begin with envy.

Stop being obsessed with what others possess. You have no right to covet what another person owns. Jesus said, "Beware, and be on your guard against every form of greed; for not even when one has an abundance does his life consist of his possessions" (Luke 12:15). Quit looking at your neighbors' property and start caring about their relationship with Christ.

2. *Trust God as your provider.*

If you view God as your true provider, you won't be bothered if someone makes more money than you or buys a nicer house than yours. God promises to meet all your needs, not all your greeds. Jesus taught us to pray, "Give us this day our *daily* bread" (Matthew 6:11). He wants us to depend upon Him every day for provision.

Trust God to supply your daily bread. He never promised to provide yearly bread. It's called "daily" because He wants you to live one day at a time. When the Israelites wandered in the wilderness for forty years, God sent bread from heaven and told them to gather only enough for one day. If they gathered more than that, it spoiled and became uneatable. The Lord was trying to teach them to trust Him every day for provision.

A rich man promised his son an annual allowance. On a certain day each year, he gave his son one lump sum. After a while the only time the man saw his son was on the day he received his allowance. He realized his son was taking him for granted.

The father decided to change the plan. Instead of giving him a large sum of money once a year, he distributed a little bit to him on a daily basis. From then on he saw his son every day.[2]

When you envy others, your eyes are focused on an earthly provider instead of your heavenly provider. Get your eyeballs off their stuff and back on God. Trust Him to provide what you need, and quit worrying about what others have.

3. *Be content with your wages.*

John the Baptist said, "Be content with your wages" (Luke 3:14). What does that mean? The Lord wants you to be happy with your salary and to live within your means. That doesn't mean you can't have a pay raise or a promotion at your job. It merely means you don't get upset when someone else gets a raise or promotion. In fact, God probably wants you to be happy for that person!

Studies by University of Illinois psychologist Ed Diener have shown that receiving a pay raise temporarily raises people's level of happiness, but then the glow fades. As people get used to having more money, they set loftier goals that often fail to produce long-term happiness. "As you start meeting basic needs, increases in income become less and less important," says Diener.[3]

Researchers found a declining effect of income on happiness at salaries well below $100,000. "Many people say, 'If I only had a million dollars, I'd be happy.' It could be true for an individual, but for most people on average, it appears not to be true."[4]

Another study has found that wealth has little effect on happiness. Dr. Diana Pidwell, a clinical psychologist, said, "It seems to be the consensus that once you have the basic level of income, then after that it does not make any difference to happiness. There is evidence that there are very wealthy people who are very unhappy. Happiness is a state of mind."[5]

Isn't happiness having the right attitude? Would you like to improve your outlook on life? Take a close look at what you already have and start thanking God for it. You've got it much better than you think.

Chapter 18

JEALOUSY

A Sneaking Suspicion

Wrath is fierce and anger is a flood,
But who can stand before jealousy? (Proverbs 27:4)

Do you remember the mythical story about Pandora's box? A man gave Pandora a mysterious box with the instructions not to open it under any circumstances. One day when she was left alone, Pandora's curiosity got the best of her. She lifted the lid to take a peek inside, and countless heartaches and miseries swarmed about her. Opening the box unleashed the sorrows of the world.

Jealousy is a Pandora's box that opens the door to more evils. James 3:16 says, "For where jealousy and selfish ambition exist, there is disorder and every evil thing." Open the door to jealousy, and other evils will follow—hate, accusations, revenge, strife, and murder, just to name a few.

What's the difference between envy and jealousy? Although they may look alike, they aren't identical twins. Envy is obsessed with possessions, while jealousy is obsessed with a person. Envy craves status; jealousy craves affection. Envy is grounded in covetousness, while jealousy is rooted in mistrust.

Jealousy is gripped with the fear that it will lose a loved one. Rooted in suspicion, it views others as threats. Insecure people accuse their loved ones of misconduct. Jealousy doesn't trust, even when the accused individual is innocent.

Let's suppose Jesus got married while He was on earth. His wife is insanely jealous, even though He is sinless. His wife says, "I saw you talking to Mary Magdalene yesterday. What were you talking about?"

"It was innocent. I was just telling her about the kingdom of God."

"Oh, is that so? I've noticed you've been talking about that to her a lot lately!"

Joseph's brothers had a problem with jealousy.

His brothers saw that their father loved him more than all his brothers; and so they hated him and could not speak to him on friendly terms. . . . His brothers were jealous of him. (Genesis 37:4, 11)

Jealousy drove them to plot his murder.

After David killed Goliath, women danced in the streets and sang victory songs. Saul smiled when they sang, "Saul has slain his thousands." He thought, *Hey, they're singing my favorite song!* Then the women sang the second stanza: "And David his ten thousands" (1 Samuel 18:7).

Saul's smile turned to scorn. *They think David is ten times better than I am. What will they call me in verse three? Saul the Chicken-Hearted?*

When Saul heard the women exalting David rather than himself, jealousy consumed him. An evil spirit came on Saul, and he "looked at David with suspicion from that day on" (1 Samuel 18:9). He wore those specs until his dying day.

King Herod executed his wife Mariamne because he suspected that she had committed adultery. When he heard the King of the Jews was born, he ordered the small children in Bethlehem to be slaughtered because he was jealous of a newborn king.

Can you see the fruit of jealousy? Accusations. Hatred. Murder.

Whether jealousy is caused by reality or imaginations, it creates tremendous tension in relationships. Years ago when I was dating the young lady who would eventually become my wife, jealous imaginations started flashing through my mind. We were in a long-distance relationship, so the devil tried planting a few doubts and suspicions.

One day as I was being tortured by these thoughts, I picked up God's Word to find help. I opened my Bible to the book of James. The following verses jumped out at me: "If you have bitter jealousy and selfish ambition in your heart, do not be arrogant and so lie against the truth. This wisdom is not that which comes down from above, but is earthly, natural, *demonic*" (James 3:14–15).

God's Word had nailed the source of my imaginations. Those tormenting thoughts of jealousy weren't true but were coming straight from the pit of hell. As soon as I realized what was happening—poof!—the demon left. My eyes were opened to the truth, and the truth set me free.

It's no wonder why the devil deposited those lying thoughts in my mind. He wanted to wreck the relationship between Cindy and me. We've been happily married and serving the Lord together for more than thirty years, and Satan wanted to keep that from happening.

Analyzing Jealousy

Jealousy arises out of actual unfaithfulness or perceived disloyalty. God wants to build holy relationships, without infidelity or jealousy. Jealousy never fixes anything but usually places a greater strain on the relationship and makes it even worse. Let's analyze this destructive attitude.

Step 1: *Jealousy gets suspicious.*

Jealousy is extremely mistrustful and will go to ridiculous lengths to confirm suspicions. Chuck Swindoll once counseled a young married couple. The husband suspected his wife was cheating on him, even though it wasn't true. The wife said, "This man is so jealous of me—before he leaves for work in the morning he checks the odometer on my car. Then when he comes home, sometimes even before he comes into the house, he checks it again. If I have driven a few extra miles, he quizzes me during supper."[1]

Imaginations are the fertilizer that makes jealousy grow. Suppose that Sally is a girl in high school who has a boyfriend. One day Betty transfers from another school, and all the guys in school are talking about how cute she is. Suddenly she wonders if her boyfriend is going to dump her for the new competition. The "jealousy movie" starts playing on the screen of her mind. Now she "sees" in her mind that her boyfriend is sneaking around with Betty. This leads to step 2.

Step 2: *Jealousy feels threatened.*

Jealousy usually involves a rival lover. A third party enters the picture, creating a threat to the relationship. The object of affection is usually a person, but not always. It could be a hobby, a sport, a car, or even a job that becomes the rival lover in the relationship.

After Sally gets suspicious that her boyfriend is attracted to the new girl, she will feel threatened. Jealousy is based on insecurity. When a person feels insecure, he or she will direct anger at whoever is perceived to be better and will start attacking the threat.

To destroy the competition, Sally starts rumors around the school about Betty. She whispers to her friends, "I heard that she sleeps around with everyone she sees. There's no telling how many diseases she has!" Betty hasn't done anything wrong, but now rumors are being spread about her, which is accepted by the gossipers as fact. Jealousy viciously attacks the competition.

John Oresky was a musician who played with some great bands and orchestras. He spent so much time playing the flute that his wife became jealous, which added to their marital problems. He gave more attention to his musical instrument than to his wife.

One day his wife decided to leave him. Oddly, she didn't remove any of the clothes from her closet when she departed. She only took one object with her—his flute. Oresky explained why his wife ran off with his instrument. "It's because she is jealous of that flute."[2]

An insecure, jealous person will view others as potential threats. This doesn't mean you should blindly trust everyone or ignore the truth. Be discerning. God wants you to protect your spouse because you have been joined together by the marriage covenant. But you need to distinguish between what is, and what isn't, a legitimate threat to the relationship.

Step 3: *Jealousy starts accusing.*

After a person gets suspicious and feels threatened, the accusations will begin. Sally now starts bombarding her boyfriend with questions. "You didn't answer your phone last night. Where were you? Were you sneaking around with Betty? I've noticed you don't seem to want me around like you used to. Are you cheating on me?"

It may or may not be true that the loved one is actually cheating in the relationship. Either way, the accused is now on trial, and it's wise to remember that a fair trial is always based on evidence, not hearsay.

Jealousy usually accuses the loved one of misconduct and says, "Guilty until proven innocent." The accused person typically defends his or her innocence. Allegations can be devastating if the accused hasn't done anything wrong. But even if the party is guilty, reacting in a jealous rage doesn't fix the problem.

The fact is—you cannot make anyone love you. You can, however, drive a loved one away by constantly making angry accusations. Instead of drawing the person closer to you, a mistrustful attitude sends the loved one running in the other direction. Ironically, the greater separation is the opposite of what jealousy intends.

Possessiveness is the wrong solution to the jealousy problem. Learn a lesson from your kitchen cupboard. More flies are caught with honey than vinegar. Sweetness attracts. Sourness repels.

Conquering the Spirit of Jealousy

Jealousy is an extremely vicious demon that torments both the suspicious person and the accused. The hateful feelings must be stopped. Accusatory thoughts want to take over your mind. Although jealousy has no right to be there, it forces itself through the door and tries to take possession of you.

There's only one way to get rid of the intruder. By a deliberate act of your will, you must evict those thoughts out of your mind. Those imaginations won't leave on their own. You must forcefully kick them out the door and forbid them from reentering the premises. Here are some ways to kill the giant of jealousy.

1. *Don't jump to conclusions.*

Jealous imaginations can deceive you. Assumptions will cause you to jump to wrong conclusions, provoking you to take actions you'll later regret.

Sam and Jacqueline Pritchard started receiving mysterious phone calls to their home in England in the middle of the night. The person on the other end never made a comment. After a long pause, he would hang up.

They changed their phone number to stop the harassing night calls. The stalker changed his tactic. He started sending them obscene and threatening anonymous letters in the mail. The couple discovered their house had been daubed with paint, and their tires had been slashed. The Pritchards became prisoners of their own home and spent a small fortune on a security system. They had no idea what they had done to deserve such cruel treatment.

After four months of unexplained terrorism, they finally met the perpetrator. Mr. Pritchard caught James McGhee, a fifty-three-year-old man, while he was damaging their car. As they looked at each other, Pritchard asked him, "Why are you doing this to us?"

The vandal responded, "Oh, no—I've got the wrong man!"

McGhee thought he was terrorizing a different man, who had been spreading rumors about him. He had looked up Pritchard's name and address in the telephone directory and assumed he was the slanderous person. He got the wrong Pritchard.[3] His erroneous assumption brought misery to the couple for four months.

When jealousy jumps to wrong conclusions, others suffer as a result. After the damage is done, it's too late. You can stop the insanity by casting down imaginations and "taking every thought captive to the obedience of Christ" (2 Corinthians 10:5).

2. *Let Jesus be your greatest love.*

Jealousy is a heart problem, so that's where it needs to be fixed. Jesus said the greatest commandment is to "love the Lord your God with all your heart, and with all your soul, and with all your mind" (Matthew

22:37). Jealousy is more obsessed with a person than the Lord, causing your affections for that person to become greater than your passion for Christ. When you love the Lord with all your heart, you will submit your emotions to His lordship. "Love is patient, love is kind and *is not jealous* . . . does not act unbecomingly, it does not seek its own, is not provoked, does not take into account a wrong suffered" (1 Corinthians 13:4–5). Human love can be extremely jealous, act inappropriately, and can be easily provoked. God's love, agape, does not fly into a rage, or yield to provocation.[4] The only way to receive agape is through a personal relationship with Jesus Christ. When Christ becomes the ruler of your heart, His love brings your emotions under control.

What is your greatest love? Whom do you think about the most? When Jesus becomes your primary love, everyone else becomes secondary. He needs to rule your heart—not jealousy.

3. *Place your loved one in God's hands.*

If you try to control your loved one's affections, you will only get frustrated because you can't do it. How can you regulate someone else's feelings when their emotions are beyond your control? You can't.

You can, however, do your best to make yourself more attractive. Do your best to make yourself more physically attractive. Don't try to become someone else, but be the best *you* that you can be. Instead of angry accusations, which will only repel the loved one, you must remain calm and be kind. Think about it. You win by wooing, not screaming.

The ultimate solution is to place your loved one in God's hands through prayer. Perhaps you're in a dating relationship and afraid of losing your boyfriend or girlfriend. Trust the Lord that He will give you what's best. Face the reality that the one you now care about may, or may not, be God's choice for you. If you lose that person, the Lord will give you someone better. Let God decide. "No good thing does He withhold from those who walk uprightly" (Psalm 84:11).

Jealousy constructs a cage around a loved one, which becomes a prison. For a dating relationship or a marriage to work correctly, that person must be *free* to love you—without your coercion or manipulations. Christ wants you to take your hands off the situation and place your loved one in His hands.

You must release your loved one from your accusations and control. Of necessity, you must open the cage door and let the prisoner go. If the loved one returns, he or she is yours. If the loved one doesn't return, the relationship wasn't meant to be. Releasing your loved one to the Lord and placing your situation in His hands will set you free from the tormenting bondage of jealousy.

The wisdom from hell produces bitter jealousy, but the wisdom from heaven produces peace and gentleness (see James 3:14–17). Which kind of wisdom do you think will make you happier?

I can tell you from personal experience: take the thoughts from heaven.

Chapter 19

DISCOURAGEMENT

The End of Your Rope

I would have despaired unless I had believed that I would see the
  goodness of the LORD
In the land of the living. (Psalm 27:13)

Do you live where never is heard an encouraging word and the skies are cloudy all day? And no one appreciates you, right?

I hear you. I've thought about checking out of my own responsibilities a few hundred times myself. Throughout the years I've watched dozens of people quit. They go into a tailspin and never seem to recover. That's not the answer.

It's easy to get discouraged when everything goes wrong and falls apart. You're ready to resign from the human race, thinking there's no reason to continue. Before you do something you might regret later, why don't you grab a cup of coffee and let's have a heart-to-heart talk.

A tree is best measured when it is down. That's true with people too. Being down doesn't mean being done. Sometimes you must get to the end of your rope to experience God in a new way.

During the 1930s, 250 men were holding the ropes to a dirigible (an airship similar to a blimp) to keep it from floating away. Suddenly a gust of wind caught one end of the dirigible, lifting it high off the ground.

Some of the men immediately let go of their ropes and fell safely to the ground. Others panicked, clinging firmly to the end of their ropes as the nose of the dirigible arose to greater heights. Several men who couldn't keep holding on fell and were seriously injured. One man, however, continued to dangle high in the air for forty-five minutes until he was rescued. Reporters later asked him how he was able to hold on to the rope for so long.

"I didn't hold on to the rope," he replied. "I just tied it around my waist and the rope held me up."

David was once at the end of his rope and learned to let God hold him up. You do remember David, don't you? You know—the sheep-tending, rock-slinging, giant-killing, wife-stealing, song-writing guy who penned the Twenty-third Psalm? He didn't spend *all* his time lying in green pastures beside still waters. Sometimes he had to walk through the valley of the shadow of death and sit at a table in the presence of his enemies.

One day when David and his men returned to the city of Ziklag, they discovered that the Amalekites had burned the city down and had taken their wives and children captive. David fell to his knees, along with the six hundred men with him, and wept until their strength was gone (1 Samuel 30:3–6).

Just when he thought things couldn't get any worse, David overheard the men whispering behind his back, "If we hadn't left our families to follow David, none of this would have happened. This is David's fault. Let's stone him and make him pay for this!"

Murphy's Law, not to be confused with Moses' Law, was in effect that day. David was fleeing from Saul's fury. His family had been kidnapped. His own soldiers were threatening to kill him. His house had been burned down. And he probably forgot to renew his fire insurance policy.

David was at the lowest point of his life. As Jed Clampett from *The Beverly Hillbillies* would say, "Lower than a snake's belly in a wagon rut." Discouragement had drained all the strength out of his heart. He had reached the end of his rope.

When Lord Horatio Nelson was fighting the Battle of Copenhagen, his senior officer, Sir Hyde Parker, also known as "Old Vinegar," hoisted the flag signaling retreat. Nelson deliberately put his telescope to his blind eye and said, "I don't see it."

If he had surrendered when it looked like defeat, he would not have captured twelve Danish ships.

I don't see defeat. Do you?

When you're fighting the Battle of Perspective, Satan will hoist his flag, trying to get you to surrender. Remember to put a blind eye to the telescope. Refuse to look at the retreat flag. Keep going forward.

David knew he couldn't keep going on. He had no friends to whisper encouraging words. His only hope was for God to have mercy on him. Charles Spurgeon said, "Sometimes God sends His mercies in a black envelope." David opened the black envelope and read this message:

Once God has spoken;
Twice I have heard this:
That power belongs to God. (Psalm 62:11)

He called out to a power higher than himself to give him strength. Like the apostle Paul, he discovered God's power is perfected in weakness (2 Corinthians 12:9).

Maybe discouragement has drained the last ounce of energy out of your heart. You're at the end of your rope. Your fingers are slipping. Does the end of your rope mean the end of your hope? Nope.

The end of your rope is the beginning of hope! It's the place where you stop trusting in you and start trusting in God. Only after you have exhausted your own strength will you discover that God's mercy and grace is sufficient for you.

The following anonymous poem gives wise counsel to those who are going through a difficult time:

When things go wrong, as they sometimes will,
When the road you're trudging seems all uphill,
When funds are low and debts are high
And you want to smile but you have to sigh,
When care is pressing you down a bit—
Rest if you must, but don't you quit.

Life is strange with its twists and turns,
As every one of us sometimes learns;
And many a failure turns about,
When he might have won had he stuck it out.
Don't give up though the pace seems slow;
You may succeed with another blow.

Often the goal is nearer than
It seems to a faint and faltering man;
Often the struggler has given up
When he might have captured the victor's cup;
And he learned too late, when the night slipped down,
How close he was to the golden crown.

Success is failure turned inside out
The silver tint in the clouds of doubt;
And you cannot tell how close you are,
It may be near when it seems afar.
So stick to the fight when you're hardest hit;
It's when things seem worst that you mustn't quit.[1]

Some people get discouraged because they've burned out. A burned-out lightbulb doesn't produce light. Neither does a burned-out Christian. Burnout is a modern-day term for "growing weary." Galatians 6:9 says, "Let us not lose heart in doing good, for in due time we shall reap if we do not grow weary."

It's so easy to quit. All we have to do is keep giving out until the tank is empty. Then when the fuel gauge reads "E," we quit. We go from giving *out* to giving *up*. Burnout occurs when we give out more than we take in. Cars that aren't refueled will run out of gas. Wells that aren't replenished will run dry. Batteries that aren't recharged will have no power. We are no different. A Christian who isn't refueled, replenished, and recharged will burn out.

Burnout is a process that occurs over time. It begins by burning the candle at both ends. Pastor Rick Warren has said, "If you are burning the candle at both ends, you are not as bright as you think you are." Constantly giving out to others will eventually bring you to the point of exhaustion. You're sapped of strength. Your motivation to continue is gone. You can't stand the thought of one more obligation, so you resign. It happens every day in jobs, marriages, and churches.

Staying Encouraged

How do you stay encouraged when you're at the end of your rope? Although you might not feel like it, you must do a few things to stay encouraged.

1. Look past your problem to the finish line.

Henry Ford once said, "Obstacles are those frightful things you see when you take your eyes off your goal." You must remember that Satan wants to keep you from reaching your destination. If you'll keep persevering, you will be rewarded. You must look past the obstacle in the road and see the finish line. Jesus looked past the cross by keeping His eyes fixed on the eternal kingdom. "For the joy set before Him" He "endured the cross" (Hebrews 12:2).

A king placed a huge boulder on a road and then hid to see if anyone would remove the obstruction. Some travelers came along and walked around it. Later others came up to it and blamed the king for not keeping the roads clear. After a while, a peasant came along. He realized the boulder would be a problem for everyone traveling on that road, so he decided to move it. He pushed on the rock with all his might, but it wouldn't budge. As he continued to press against the boulder, it slowly began to roll. After an hour of straining, he finally pushed it off the road.

When he turned around, he noticed a bag lying where the rock had been. Inside the purse he discovered gold coins and a note from the king. It read, "This reward goes to the person who persevered and moved the boulder off the path."

The obstacles in your path are placed there to see if you really want something or just thought you did. Don't get discouraged or give up.

Sometimes the reward isn't always apparent because a boulder is covering it up. You won't receive your prize until you've overcome and finished the task.

Remember that the problem you face will never be more than the grace God will give you to handle it. "But He gives a greater grace" (James 4:6).

2. Don't lose your confidence.

Keep your composure during difficult times because confidence promises a great reward. "Therefore, do not throw away your confidence, which has a great reward. For you have need of endurance, so that when you have done the will of God, you may receive what was promised" (Hebrews 10:35–36). The giant of discouragement wants you to throw away your confidence so you'll forfeit the reward.

I've never met a confident discouraged person. If you took a vote of confidence, the nays would have it. It's hard to endure trying times without being empowered by the Holy Spirit.

Several children in a park watched a man release helium-filled balloons. The man let go of a white balloon, which floated up into the sky. Then he released yellow and red balloons, which also flew up and away.

A little black boy asked, "Mister, if you let go of a black balloon, will it go up?"

The man replied, "Son, the color on the outside has nothing to do with it. It's what's on the inside that makes it go up."

When God's Spirit fills your heart, you will be lifted up and will confidently rise above the clouds of discouragement.

3. Receive encouragement from other believers.

It's hard to pedal your bike if the tires are flat. Discouragement is like having leaky tires. You're deflated because all the wind has gone out of you. The way to fix your bike is by pumping up the tires. And if you'll pump up your spirit, you'll be encouraged and your discouragement will go away.

God knows we all need encouragement, so He designed His church to be a filling station for deflated and discouraged souls. Hebrews 10:25 says, "Not forsaking our own assembling together, as is the habit of some, but encouraging one another." One of the purposes of the church is to pump people up so they will stay encouraged. Enthusiasm is contagious, and you can catch it from other believers.

But if you withdraw from the fellowship of other believers, it opens the door for you to get discouraged. Your spirit starts leaking, but no one is there to pump you up. Some people never figure out that their choice to isolate themselves is the cause of their discouragement.

You may have pulled away from church because something went wrong while you were there. But that doesn't mean all churches are that way. Don't paint all churches with the same broad brush. The solution is to carefully look for a healthy fellowship of believers and get plugged in there. If you know a Christian who is filled with joy and is enthusiastic about life, ask where that person goes to church, and then visit there. If you'll find a group of encouraging believers to fellowship with, it will help you tremendously.

4. Don't stop knocking on closed doors.

Many of God's blessings are waiting behind doors that are yet to be knocked on. God wants you to be persistent. Keep asking. Keep seeking. Keep knocking. Jesus said, "Ask, and it will be given to you; seek, and you will find; knock, and it will be opened to you" (Matthew 7:7).

You'll never know which door has the treasure on the other side until you knock on the right one. It could be door number 99. Discouragement tries to convince you the door will never open, so you might as well turn around and go home.

Late one afternoon when the office was about to close, a business manager finally allowed a life insurance salesman to see him. The manager told the salesman, "You should feel highly honored. Do you know that I have refused to see seven insurance men today?"

"I know," replied the agent. "I'm them."

God loves to bless those who keep knocking after everyone else has clocked out and gone home. Because most people are looking for shortcuts, persistence is the most overlooked means of receiving God's blessings. It is the long, hard way to receive good things from God, and most people aren't willing to take that route.

Scientists have proven the power of persistence through an experiment using an iron ball and a cork. A one-ton iron ball was suspended from the ceiling using a metal cable. A small cork hung by a thread next to the heavy ball. An electrical mechanism kept the cork gently bouncing against the iron weight.

After many days of constant pounding by the cork, the researchers noticed the iron ball starting moving ever so slightly. The cork continued to knock against it until the heavy ball swung widely back and forth on its own.

Although you might think that you aren't making progress, the door will open if you will keep knocking. Your persistent faith will be the difference in moving the mountain in your life.

5. *Remember that God always has the last word.*

God may not have caused the difficulty you are currently experiencing, but He does have the last word. The Lord is still on His throne, no matter how gloomy things may appear. You can still have hope, even when things don't go the way you think they should.

I don't understand why some things happen the way they do, but I do know God causes all things to work together for good to those who love Him (see Romans 8:28). Knowing that God determines the outcome gives me encouragement to keep going when times get rough.

It kept David going too. After he strengthened himself in the Lord, he rallied the troops together, conquered the Amalekites, and recovered everything they had taken. That would not have been possible if he had let discouragement talk him into quitting.

Now that we've had our little talk, are you feeling better? Take a look outside. The sun is shining, the antelope are playing, and I don't hear any more discouraging words.

I hope you now understand that the end of your rope doesn't mean the end of your hope. It's the beginning of a new adventure with God.

Chapter 20

DEATH

Scared to Death

> Yet you do not know what your life will be like tomorrow. You are just a vapor that appears for a little while and then vanishes away. (James 4:14)

Anthony Fernando, a twenty-one-year-old man living in Colombo, Sri Lanka, went fishing one day off the coast of the island. He had no idea he would never make it back alive. If you would venture to guess how this man lost his life, what would you say? That he died from a heart attack? Perhaps he fell out of the boat and drowned? How about a shark attack?

It was none of these things. A forktail gar fish jumped out of the water and cut him on the neck with its tail. He bled to death before a fellow fisherman could get him to a hospital.[1] If you had told him that morning that a fish would kill him, he wouldn't have believed it.

If you would have told Ali-Asghar Ahani he would be killed by a snake, he might have believed it. But not in the way it happened. Although he could have shot the snake, this man from Iran was trying to capture it alive. When he pressed the butt of his shotgun behind its head, the snake coiled itself around the gun. With its tail thrashing, the snake pulled the trigger, firing one of the barrels.[2] Ahani was shot to death by the snake, which used his own gun as a weapon.

John Bowen wasn't expecting to die when he attended a Jets-Patriots football game. Did he die of heat stroke? Was he trampled by overly zealous fans? Neither.

At halftime, the entertainment was a performance of radio-controlled, unusual-looking model airplanes that flew around the stadium. One of the planes, a flying lawnmower, went out of control and flew into the stands where Bowen was seated.[3] He has gone down in history as the only person ever to be killed by a flying lawnmower during a football game.

A herdsman was watering his cattle at a pool in eastern Kenya when a group of wild monkeys started throwing stones at him. One of the rocks hit him in the head, which caused the injury that led to his death.[4] If you had told him that he would die from rocks thrown by angry monkeys, he never would have believed you.

None of these people believed that death was just moments away. Death can come unexpectedly to anyone, and one day your time will come.

Have you ever thought about how you will die? Will you be cut by a fish tail? Shot by a snake? Killed by a flying lawnmower? Stoned by wild monkeys? Maybe your heart will just stop beating. You probably won't be able to predict how or when your demise will occur. Nevertheless, you have an appointment with the coffin. You have a one-way ticket to the grave and the fact that you are getting older is a reminder that the train hasn't stopped.

Everyone is biodegradable. Statistics show one out of every one person is going to die. It's coming, like it or not. When your turn comes, you need to be prepared. No, you can do better than that. You can actually look forward to it.

The Fear of Death

The fear of death is the greatest of all fears. King Louis XV of France was so afraid of death that he ordered the word *death* never to be spoken in his presence. He believed if no one mentioned death, perhaps it wouldn't happen to him. It didn't work. He still died.

People are afraid of dying because they don't know what lies beyond the grave. Actually, it's the fear of God's judgment that makes most people afraid to die. Judgment can be a terrifying thing for people who don't know the Lord.

When W. C. Fields was on his deathbed, a visitor found him reading the Bible. The visitor asked why he was reading it, and Fields replied, "Looking for loopholes, my friend. Looking for loopholes." He didn't find any, but at least he found the right book to answer his questions about the afterlife. When people face death, they instinctively know where to go to find the answers.

Not everyone is afraid of death. The pagan philosopher Sinicia realized that Christians died differently than non-Christians. He once stated, "Only Christians and idiots are not afraid to die." Those who have trusted Jesus to save them have been delivered from the fear of death.

> Since the children share in flesh and blood, He Himself likewise also partook of the same, that through death He might render powerless him who had the power of death, that is, the devil, and might free those who through fear of death were subject to slavery all their lives. (Hebrews 2:14–15)

When Jesus Christ is Lord of your life, He will give you the grace to face death. W. E. Sangster, an English Methodist preacher, was on his deathbed. He wrote to his friend Billy Graham this note of hope. "All my life I have preached that Jesus Christ is adequate for every crisis. I have but a few days to live, and Billy, Christ is indeed adequate in the hour of death. Tell everyone it is true."[5] God places a supernatural peace and confidence within each believer that calms the fear of death.

In the early fourth century, a believer named Phocas lived outside the city of Sinope. He often welcomed travelers into his house to share his faith with them. During the reign of the Emperor Diocletian, an order was issued that all Christians were to be put to death. The name Phocas of Sinope was high on the list provided by the magistrates.

The officers of the magistrates, weary from a long day's journey, arrived at Sinope. Phocas welcomed them into his home and asked them their business in the area.

The commanding officer told him, "We have orders from Rome to execute a local Christian named Phocas. Do you know him and where he lives?"

"I know him well," Phocas replied. "Why don't you and your men rest for the night, and I will direct you to him in the morning."

When the men from Rome retired for the evening, Phocas went into his garden and started digging. By sunrise, the hole he had dug was large enough to bury a human body. When the Roman soldiers awoke, he told them, "I am Phocas, the man you are looking for."

The soldiers were shocked when he revealed his identity. "I am a Christian," he said, "and I'm not afraid to die. You must do your duty." Phocas was executed and buried in the grave that he had dug in his own garden.[6]

He wasn't afraid of death because he knew where his spirit would go after they killed him. Once you are assured that your spirit will be received by Jesus into heaven, the fear of death will leave.

What Happens When You Die

God didn't create you to live forever in your body on this planet. He made you to last for eternity, but you must first live on earth for a little while. Your body is like a space suit worn by the astronauts when they walked on the moon. The suits enabled them to live on the moon while they were away from earth. When they returned from their mission, they didn't need the space suits any longer.

When you go to someone's funeral, you are looking at the space suit that is not inhabited anymore. Nobody is inside that body. It is a vacant shell—an empty house. The real person has left the body.

One young minister was doing his first funeral. He explained to the congregation that the spirit departs from the body when a person dies. He then pointed to the corpse in the open casket and said, "Folks, what you see here is just a shell. The nut has already departed."

Perhaps those weren't the best choice of words, but the point is clearly illustrated: when a person dies, the spirit departs from the body. James 2:26 tells us the body without the spirit is dead. The spirit lives on after death and enters into eternity, while the body is left behind and returns to dust. Death doesn't stop your existence. It's the door through which you must go to exit this world and enter the next world.

God wants everyone to be saved (1 Timothy 2:4), and that includes you. He doesn't want anyone to go to hell, but for everyone to change their hearts and come to him (2 Peter 3:9). Even though He wants you to go to heaven, He can't save you if you reject His provision through Christ's death. Jesus is the only way to heaven (John 14:6).

Christ paid for your sins when He died on the cross, but if you refuse to accept Him as your Lord, you must pay the debt yourself. Hell is a place where people pay for their sins throughout eternity because the debt will never be paid off. However, if you will receive Christ into your life, your sin debt is paid by Jesus on your behalf. You escape God's judgment and pass from death into life. Instead of going to hell to pay for your sins, you will be saved and will spend eternity with God in heaven.

When a Christian Dies

Passing through death's door is a terrifying thought. What will it be like? Jesus said death for the Christian is like sleeping. It doesn't hurt when you go to sleep. In fact, many people look forward to going to sleep.

When Jesus rose from the dead, He took the sting out of death for all who follow Him. "O death, where is your victory? O death, where is your sting?" (1 Corinthians 15:55). Just as a bee loses its stinger when it stings, death lost its sting when it stung Jesus.

A little boy asked his mother what death was like. She said, "Do you remember when you fell asleep in the living room? Your father picked you up and carried you to your bedroom. When you woke up, you found yourself in another room. Death for a Christian is like that. You go to sleep in one room and wake up in another room. You fall asleep on earth and wake up in heaven."

Paul said he had "the desire to depart and be with Christ, for that is very much better" (Philippians 1:23). Life in heaven will be so much more exciting than life on earth. Once you grasp the incredible joy that

Jesus promised in the next life, it will destroy your fear of death. Imagine having no pain, stress, or misery. God has exciting job assignments in heaven for those who have faithfully served Him during their lives on earth. These jobs will be without stress, like having eternal hobbies. This is why Paul said he preferred to be in heaven with Christ than to remain on earth.

If you are a believer in Jesus Christ, you don't need to fear death. The sting of death is gone. A place has been reserved in heaven for you. And Jesus is on the other side, ready to welcome you into your eternal home.

Jesus Died for Your Sins

When Jesus died on the cross two thousand years ago, He died for the sins of the entire world. "He is the atoning sacrifice for our sins, and not only for our sins but also for the sins of the whole world" (1 John 2:2 NIV). As He was dying, He did something in the spiritual realm that was not visible to the human eye. The people watching Jesus die couldn't see that all the sins of the world were being placed in Him. "And He Himself bore our sins in His body on the cross" (1 Peter 2:24). That means He bore *your* sins on the cross.

His sacrificial death also stretched outside of time. With one hand He gathered all the sins committed in the past, and with the other hand He reached into the future and gathered all sins that were going to be committed, and placed them inside Himself. "But He, having offered one sacrifice for sins *for all time*, sat down at the right hand of God" (Hebrews 10:12). On that day, Jesus paid the price for your salvation. Once you grasp what happened on the cross, you will never be the same.

The archbishop of Paris was once preaching to a large congregation in Notre Dame Cathedral. He told the story of three godless men who wandered into the cathedral one day. Two of them bet the third man that he wouldn't make a confession to the priest. He accepted the bet.

During the confession, he made up an outrageous story about a sin he had committed. When he finished, the priest said, "Go to that crucifix, kneel down before it, and repeat three times, 'All this You did for me, and I don't really care.'"

The young man did what the priest asked. He kneeled down, looked up, and said, "All this You did for me, and I . . ."

Suddenly it hit him. He realized that Jesus had died for him. His heart was pierced with conviction and shame. As tears rolled down his cheeks, he prayed, "God, please forgive me. I now realize You gave Your life for me, so I'm giving my life to You."

The archbishop finished his sermon and closed his Bible. Just before he walked away, he told the congregation, "One more thing you need to know. I was that young man."[7]

People who look at the cross and walk away unchanged don't see what happened there. Do you really see what Jesus did for you?

Even though Christ paid for your sins, you must receive the free gift of salvation or it will never be yours. Ephesians 2:8–9 says, "For by grace you have been saved through faith; and that not of yourselves, it is *the gift* of God; not as a result of works, so that no one may boast." Salvation is the gift that Jesus purchased for you through His death.

Let's say someone buys an expensive gift and brings it to you. He or she holds out the present for you to take. Although the gift has been paid for, it's not yours until you reach out and take it. For a purchased gift to be transferred from one person to another, it must be *received* by the intended recipient. God will never force you to take it.

Some people think they must do something to earn the gift. They attempt to earn their salvation by attending church, confessing sins, being baptized, taking communion, and giving money. All those things are good but will never be good enough to purchase your salvation. "Now to the one who works, his wage is not credited as a favor, but as what is due. But to the one who *does not work, but believes* in Him who justifies the ungodly, his faith is reckoned as righteousness" (Romans 4:4–5).

A gift ceases to be a gift if you even add one penny to pay for it. It becomes something you have purchased and is not a free gift. If you could do something to purchase your salvation, you would become your own savior, which is impossible. There can't be two saviors—you and Jesus. He is the only Savior.

If you are drowning and someone saves you, that person becomes your savior. In the same way, you are drowning in the sea of sin, and

Jesus is the only one who can save you. How do you get saved? Just like when you are drowning—you call out to Him to save you.

How to Be Saved

Romans 10:13 says, "Whoever will call on the name of the Lord will be saved." You call upon His name through prayer. If you would like to follow Christ and be forgiven of your sins, you can say this prayer:

Heavenly Father, I admit to You that I'm a sinner and need to be saved. Lord Jesus, thank You for sacrificing Your life on the cross for my sins. Please come into my life and save me. I give You my life, and I will follow You the rest of my days. Take me to heaven when I die. Thank You for saving me! Amen.

Now I ask you, did He come into your life? Yes, He did. He promised that He would (Revelation 3:20). If you sincerely prayed that prayer, you are now a Christian. Because you now have eternal life, you don't need to be afraid of dying. "These things I have written to you who believe in the name of the Son of God, so that you may know that you have eternal life" (1 John 5:13).

Now He wants to live His life through you. Tell someone that you have received Jesus into your life. Read at least one chapter of the Bible every day. Find a church that preaches God's Word and get involved there.

I might not ever meet you on earth, but I will be excited to meet you in heaven!

DISCUSSION GUIDE FOR GROUP STUDIES

Chapter 1

HOPELESSNESS
One in a Billion

Read Matthew 17:24–27. What are three things Jesus knew before they happened?

Read Psalm 139:1–4. What are five things God knows about you?

If God knows our needs before we ask Him, why should we pray?

Why did Jesus tell Peter to use a hook rather than a net to catch the fish? What does this tell us about God's ability to control circumstances?

How does this apply to the problems we face every day?

Read Genesis 22:10–14. What are some things we learn from this about God's provision and divine appointments?

Do you think Abraham was expecting God to provide a ram? (See Hebrews 11:17–19.)

What is the correlation between obedience and provision?

From our perspective, how do the odds of something happening affect our faith? From God's perspective, does He have to consider the odds?

What is the hopeless situation you are praying about? How has this chapter helped to build your faith?

Chapter 2

FEAR

How's Your Nervous System?

What are your greatest fears?

Faith and fear are both assumptions about the future. What does faith assume? What does fear assume?

Read Psalm 23:4. How can being aware of God's presence help you overcome fear?

Read Matthew 8:23–26. How does the amount of faith you have affect the amount of fear you experience?

Share a situation where you panicked like the disciples. What will you do differently the next time a storm comes your way?

Read Psalm 56:3–4. What does it mean to "put" your trust in God? Is it possible to put your trust in God and be afraid at the same time?

What does the story about floating on water illustrate about how to trust God?

Read Psalm 91:5–10, which speaks of being afraid of the "terror by night" and "of the arrow that flies by day." What would be some modern-day examples?

What does Psalm 91:1–2 tell us to do to overcome our fears?

In the story about the overnight campout, what brought peace into the tent during the electrical storm?

Chapter 3

DISCONTENTMENT
May I Change Seats, Please?

How can discontentment be manifested? Name several ways.

Read Philippians 4:11–12. How did Paul learn how to be content in every circumstance? What is the correlation between learning something and applying it to life?

Paul learned "the secret" of being content. Name some facts about secrets.

Paul believed God assigned him a seat in prison. What does this say about God's control over your unpleasant circumstances?

How does the way you view your circumstances influence your contentment?

The grizzly bear has chosen to coexist with the skunk. Discuss how you can get along with the skunk in your life.

Why does the grass always look greener somewhere else? What is life like "on the other side of the fence" after you get there?

Why is it necessary to be happy with what you already have before you can enjoy the new things you receive?

What does it mean to "play the cards that have been dealt to you"?

What is necessary to enjoy the trip through life?

Chapter 4

DOUBT
Without a Doubt

What are some things that cause you to doubt?

Read James 1:5–8. What is the primary characteristic of doubt? How does doubt affect us when we're making decisions?

Read Matthew 14:28–31. When Peter was walking on the water, what caused him to doubt?

Why do you think circumstances can cause us to waver in our faith?

When Jesus sent a message back to John the Baptist, why did Jesus quote those Scriptures?

Read John 9:1, 6–8, 18–21, 25. The former blind man said, "One thing I do know." Why is it important to concentrate on what you do know rather than what you don't know?

Read Proverbs 3:5. What does it mean to lean on your own understanding?

How can you keep trusting God, even when you don't have all your questions answered?

Why is it important to trust God's Word to guide us through life?

Chapter 5

TEMPTATION

Adam and Eve's Instruction Manual

What did Jesus mean when He said, "Lead us not into temptation" (Luke 11:4)?

What happens to us after we "enter into" temptation?

How does the statement "It is hard to pick fruit if you are a hundred yards away, but it is easy at an arm's length" apply to us today?

Read Matthew 26:41. Why does "trying not to do it" never work?

Read 2 Timothy 2:22. Why is running away from temptation better than trying to resist it?

What does it mean to have your "eyes opened" after you have sinned?

If Adam and Eve had been eating of the legitimate fruit from the trees God had provided for them, they would not have been hungry for the forbidden fruit. How does this apply to fulfilling our needs today?

How can an accountability partner with whom you regularly meet keep you from falling into temptation?

Read 1 Corinthians 10:13. What does it mean that God will make a way of escape?

Read Galatians 5:16–17. What does it mean to walk in the Spirit? How can walking in the Spirit keep you from fulfilling the desires of your flesh?

Chapter 6

UNFORGIVENESS

Who Is in Your Dungeon?

Read Matthew 18:23–30. The king forgave him from the fifty-million-dollar debt. Why do you think the first slave forgot how much he had been forgiven?

How did the king respond when he heard that the first slave would not forgive his fellow slave? How does this apply to us when we don't forgive?

What does it mean to base your forgiveness on what God has done for you and not what someone did to you?

Read Luke 6:35. What does Jesus promise to those who will love their enemies and expect nothing in return?

The king felt compassion for the slave who owed him the debt (Matthew 18:27). What does it mean to feel compassion? Why is feeling compassion for your enemies an important ingredient in forgiving them?

When we forgive, we choose to take responsibility for the debt the person owes us. What is the proof that we have done this and have truly forgiven?

What happens to us every time we replay the hurt on the DVR in our minds? How can we stop thinking about what the person did to us?

Do you have anyone in the dungeon of your soul? How can you release and let go of that person(s)?

What happens to us when we truly forgive others?

Chapter 7

GUILT

Canceling Guilt Trips

Read Matthew 27:20–25. Why do you think Pilate washed his hands?

How did Adam and Eve use the blame-it-on-someone-else method? Why do guilty people tend to blame others?

Why does guilt drive people away from fellowshipping with other believers?

If you know someone who has dropped out of church or fellowship, what might possibly be an underlying reason?

Explain how Judas used the deny-and–cover-up method at the Last Supper in the upper room. How is this method related to hypocrisy?

Read Psalm 32:5. Why is confession the first step in canceling guilt trips?

If someone buys you a gift, what is the only thing required of you? How does this apply to God's offering forgiveness to you?

How can a person receive something he or she can't see?

How does the "remember the duck" story relate to the lies of Satan?

What happens when the blood of Christ encounters sin?

Chapter 8

CHANGE

Breaking Out of Comfort Zones

What is a comfort zone? What specifically are your comfort zones?

Change is the greatest threat to a comfort zone. What are some reasons people don't like change?

Why does breaking out of a comfort zone make you feel uncomfortable?

Read Matthew 14:28–29. Breaking out of a comfort zone requires a step of faith. What must happen before we can have faith to take that step (Romans 10:17)?

Using the analogy of Peter's feet and the boat, explain the difference between unbelief, doubt, and faith.

What should be our primary motive for making any kind of change?

Why did Peter sink after walking on the water?

What did Jesus do when Peter went under water? How does this apply to us when we try something new?

What are some of the blessings on the other side of the comfort zone?

Chapter 9

WORRY

The Movies in Your Mind

At the beginning of the chapter, why did the people imitate what they had seen at the movies?

The package delivery driver's wife acted on what she believed to be true. Discuss the statement: "We act, not necessarily upon truth, but on what we *believe* to be true."

The Bible teaches that Satan has the ability to plant thoughts and suggestions in our minds. What happens to us when we allow imaginations to control our thinking?

Read 2 Corinthians 10:5. We can stop the movies from playing in our minds by casting down the imagination. What does it mean to "cast down" an imagination? How can we do it?

How do we "take every thought captive" to the obedience of Christ (2 Corinthians 10:5)?

Read Philippians 4:6. How can prayer keep us from worrying?

Read Matthew 6:31–34. What were the people of that day worried about? What do people today worry about the most?

What did Jesus promise if we would seek first God's kingdom and His righteousness (Matthew 6:33)?

How can learning to live one day at a time keep us from worrying?

Do you think God wants us to enjoy life (John 15:11)?

Chapter 10

SELF-IMAGE

I Love Me, I Love Me Not

The word *hate* doesn't always mean to "cease loving." What does it mean in Luke 14:26?

According to author Leanne Payne, why is it dangerous to hate the soul that God loves?

Read Numbers 13:32–33. The spies compared themselves and said, "We became like grasshoppers in our own sight, and so we were in their sight." Why does the way you view yourself determine how you think others view you?

Define "self-image." How can a warped self-image be compared to the crazy house of mirrors at the carnival?

Which of the following have you used to determine your self-image? Physical appearance, intelligence, abilities, success. Why is this wrong?

What are the two different ways "self" can be defined? When Jesus said to hate your own life (Luke 14:26), do you think He meant the person God made you to be or that you are to hate selfishness?

What is the difference between Jesus commanding you to love your neighbor "as yourself" (Matthew 22:39) and Paul's warning against being a "lover of self" (2 Timothy 3:2)?

Read Romans 9:20. What does this teach us about accepting ourselves as God's creation?

Read Psalm 139:13–14. How does this verse apply to self-image?

Why is it important not to view others as competition?

Chapter 11

PESSIMISM

Treasure Hunting

How is perspective like having a cameraman inside your heart?

In the story about the hot dog salesman, how can a negative attitude create a depressing world to live in?

Read Genesis 37:5–8. Joseph's brothers interpreted his dream but failed to see God's hand in the dream. Why are they an example of pessimism?

Using the example of the dot on the piece of paper, explain how we can leave God out of the picture.

Do you think that Karl Wallenda's negative focus contributed to his accident? How does pessimism affect our confidence?

Why is complaining a proof of a pessimistic attitude?

Read Philippians 4:8. List the different kinds of thoughts that should occupy our minds.

Kent sold his joy for seven dollars. Give an example of when you exchanged your joy.

Read 1 Thessalonians 5:18. How can being continually thankful change our attitudes?

Roy Parrino found treasure in the sewer. Give an example of when you found something good when you were in a bad situation.

Chapter 12

ANGER

Anger Mismanagement

What causes anger?

Read Proverbs 16:32. Why is ruling your own spirit more important than controlling a city?

Read Ephesians 4:26–27. What happens to your anger if you don't resolve it before the day is over?

Read Mark 3:3–5. Why is it important for your anger to be mixed with grief?

How can lowering your expectations of others help you deal with your anger?

Read Genesis 4:3–6. Why did God ask Cain the reason he was angry? Why is it important to identify the cause of your anger?

Read Genesis 4:7–8. What did God tell Cain to do to control his anger?

Read Proverbs 15:1. How can lowering your tone of voice calm the anger in others?

What does it mean to accept those things that you can't change? How can this keep you from getting angry?

Read Ephesians 4:31–32. How can you divorce yourself from anger?

Chapter 13

REJECTION
The Angel Inside the Marble

Rejection isn't what happens to us, but *how we interpret* what happens to us. Explain why.

Why didn't anyone greet the pastor's friend after the church service? Explain why some people cause their own rejection.

Discuss the story about the woman wearing the nice dress. Explain how our imaginations can cause rejection.

Read Romans 14:3. Why is it vital to find our acceptance in God?

Read Matthew 10:14. Why did Jesus tell His disciples to shake the dust off their feet before they left town?

Discuss how God sometimes uses rejection as a closed door to protect you from harm.

Read Genesis 50:20. When Joseph looked back over his life, how did he view his brothers' rejection of him? Do you think we can view our rejections in the same way?

Read Romans 12:18. Why should you attempt to make peace with those who reject you?

In what ways did God change George after he made an attempt to make peace with the father who had rejected him?

Chapter 14

IMPATIENCE
God's Waiting Room

When Sarai failed to get pregnant after ten years, why did she tell her husband Abram to have a child through Hagar (Genesis 16:1–3)?

Read Genesis 17:18–19. Why do you think God had Abraham and Sarah wait twenty-five years before Isaac was born?

What was Saul's excuse for not waiting for Samuel to offer the burnt offering (1 Samuel 10:8: 13:8–12)? What was the penalty for his impatience (1 Samuel 13:13–14)?

What does restlessness and irritability reveal about our spiritual condition?

Sometimes we must wait because we're not ready for what God has for us. What would have been the consequences if Hannah had started driving too soon?

What should a single person do while he or she is waiting to get married?

Sometimes what God has planned for us may not be ready. Ecclesiastes 3:1 says, "There is an appointed time for everything." What does this tell us about God's timing and His control of circumstances?

Read Romans 4:20–21. What happened to Abraham's faith as he continued to wait on the Lord?

Using the illustration of lifting weights, how does patience make life easier for us?

Read Psalm 37:3–7. Paraphrase the four things we must do while waiting.

Trust in the Lord

_____

Delight yourself in the Lord

_____

Commit your way to the Lord

_____

Rest in the Lord

_____

Chapter 15

BURDENS

Check Your Baggage Here

What is a burden and where do we carry it?

How can burdens be compared to carrying luggage?

How do we accumulate excess baggage and how does it affect us?

When you go to an airport, why do they check your baggage? How does this apply to the baggage you carry on your soul?

Where is the only place "the past" exists? How can you tell if a person is living in the past?

How does a person carry future baggage? Why is worrying "negative faith"?

What are some things that produce stress in your life?

Read Luke 10:38–42. Why was Martha worried and bothered? What did Jesus say to do?

Read 1 Peter 5:7. What is necessary to cast a ball to someone? How does this apply to casting our burdens to the Lord?

How do you know if you have let go of a problem?

How can you wisely plan for the future without being preoccupied with the future?

Chapter 16

DEPRESSION

Singing in the Dark

Read 1 Kings 19:1–4. How do you think Elijah felt when Jezebel sent him the death threat? How do we view our problems when we are depressed?

When we get depressed, which person is the one we think about the most? How can this compound the problem?

Why does depression cause us to lose hope for the future? Do you think this hopelessness is real or imagined? Why?

Take the Thought-Analyzer Test. Discuss how our thoughts affect our emotions.

What is the cause for most depression? How can changing the way we think also change the way we feel?

According to the study done by Dr. Michael Jacobson, how did thinking negatively affect patients' bodies? How did thinking positively affect their bodies? How do these results apply to depression?

Read Philippians 4:4. How often should we rejoice? Why is it important to verbalize our thoughts through thanksgiving, rejoicing, and praising?

Read Proverbs 17:22. Why is a joyful heart like good medicine?

Read Psalm 27:13 and Psalm 42:5. When we are depressed, why is it important to regain our hope?

Read Psalm 42:8. Why is singing praise and worship to God important during times when we are depressed?

How does reaching out and helping others also help alleviate depression?

Chapter 17

ENVY

The Possession Obsession

In the parable of the vineyard workers (Matthew 20:1–15), why were some of the workers upset at what the others got paid? Share an example when you've been upset at someone else's salary.

Envy begins by comparing what we have with what someone else has. What are some of the things that we compare?

Read Exodus 20:17. What does it mean to "covet" what your neighbor has? How does this apply to "keeping up with the Joneses"?

Discuss how Kent learned *not* to covet Robbie's hamburger in his head but *to* covet it in his heart. If "head knowledge" isn't enough to correct the envy problem, what will fix it? (See Mark 7:21–22.)

What did the all-day workers do when the one-hour workers were paid the same amount (Matthew 20:11)? How are modern-day laborers guilty of the same thing?

Read James 4:1–2. What was the source of their quarrels and conflicts? Do you think this is also the cause of conflicts today?

What does it mean to love your neighbor and not what your neighbor has?

How can viewing God as your provider keep you from being envious of what others have?

Explain what "being content with your wages" means and what it doesn't mean.

Chapter 18

JEALOUSY

A Sneaking Suspicion

Explain the differences between envy and jealousy.

Jealousy can be based on a real or imagined violation of trust. Why does mistrust create jealousy?

When Betty transferred from another school, why did Sally suddenly feel threatened? Is a jealous person secure or insecure?

Jealousy leads to accusations, where the loved one is put on trial. In our justice system, what is the difference between real evidence and hearsay? How does this apply to jealous accusations?

Although jealousy tries to make the loved one come closer, why does it do just the opposite?

Can you make anyone love you? What is the kitchen-cupboard lesson we can learn about honey and vinegar?

What can we learn about jumping to conclusions from the Sam Pritchard story?

Read Matthew 22:37. Do you think that jealousy is more obsessed with a person than the Lord? What can be done to change that?

Read James 3:14–17. Where do jealous imaginations come from? What does the wisdom from above produce in our hearts?

How can you put your loved one in God's hands?

Chapter 19

DISCOURAGEMENT
The End of Your Rope

Read 1 Samuel 30:1–6. What were some of the bad things that happened to David to discourage him? What did David do to overcome his discouragement (v. 6)?

What did the apostle Paul discover when he was weak (2 Corinthians 12:9)?

Read Galatians 6:9. What does it mean to "lose heart"? What does God promise if we will keep going and not grow weary?

What lessons can we learn from the story of the king who placed the boulder in the road?

Read Hebrews 12:2. What did Jesus look forward to as He was dying on the cross? How can we look past our current discouraging circumstances?

Read Hebrews 10:25. What happens to us when we withdraw from Christian fellowship? What happens to us when we are fellowshipping with believers who love us?

Read Hebrews 10:35–36. Why is it so important for us to keep our confidence during a trial?

Read Matthew 7:7. Why is it important to keep persevering when we are discouraged?

What truth is demonstrated in the experiment of the iron ball and cork? How does this apply to persistent faith?

Read Romans 8:28. What does it mean that "God has the last word"?

Chapter 20

DEATH

Scared to Death

Read the four stories about the unusual deaths. What did all four cases have in common?

What are some reasons people are afraid of dying?

According to Hebrews 2:14–15, what two things did Jesus accomplish through His death on the cross?

Do you think God wants His children to be afraid of death? Why or why not?

How can our bodies be compared to space suits like those worn by the astronauts when they walked on the moon?

Read 1 Timothy 2:4. How many people does God want to save? Does that include you?

Read 1 Corinthians 15:51. What did Jesus do to death through His resurrection? How can the death of a Christian be compared to going to sleep in a room?

Read Philippians 1:23. Why did Paul say the next life in heaven would be better than this life?

Read 1 Peter 2:24. Sin keeps us away from God, but what did Jesus do for you on the cross?

Read Ephesians 2:8–9. If someone buys you a gift and offers it to you, what is the only thing left to complete the transaction?

Read Romans 10:13. Have you called on the Lord to save you? If not, sincerely say the prayer in this chapter. When you do, you will no longer be afraid to die.

NOTES

Chapter 1: Hopelessness

1. *Faith & Renewal*, March/April 1993, 29.
2. Raymond McHenry, *The Best of In Other Words*, (Author, 1996), 32–22. Note: I have talked with Gene Alexander and he verified that this story is accurate.
3. David Smith was my roommate when I attended Southwestern Baptist Theological Seminary.
4. Franklin Graham, "When the Lights Went On," in *Snowflakes in September* (Nashville: Dimensions for Living, 1992), 38.

Chapter 2: Fear

1. Max Wilkins is the senior pastor of The Family Church in Gainesville, Florida.
2. Bruce Larson, *The Presence* (San Francisco: Harper & Row, 1988), 10–11.
3. *USA Today*, October 23, 1989.
4. *Quote*, August 1992, 248.

Chapter 3: Discontentment

1. Jack Hyles, *Revival Fires!*, April 1995, 6.
2. Ann Landers, *Garden City Telegram*, September 30, 1996, B-10.
3. Phil is a friend of mine but I have changed his name.

Chapter 5: Temptation

1. Paul Lee Tan, *Encyclopedia of 7700 Illustrations* (Rockville, MD: Assurance, 1979), 1534.

Chapter 6: Unforgiveness

1. Carl Windsor, *On This Day* (Nashville: Thomas Nelson, 1989), 93.

Chapter 7: Guilt

1. *Reader's Digest*, September 1991, 32.
2. *Our Daily Bread* (Grand Rapids: Radio Bible Class Ministries).
3. Cited in *Leadership,* Fall 1983, 86.

Chapter 8: Change

1. Don McCullough, "Reasons to Fear Easter," in *Preaching Today*, Tape 116.
2. Walter Knight, *Knight's Master Book of New Illustrations* (Grand Rapids: Eerdmans, 1956), 510.

Chapter 9: Worry

1. "Violent Film Inspired Teens, Police Say," *Detroit News*, March 25, 1994.
2. "Movie May Have Influenced Teen to Kill," United Press International, March 7, 1995.
3. "Cruise Ships on Lookout for 'Titanic' Copycats," Associated Press, June 24, 1998.

Chapter 10: Self-Image

1. Leanne Payne, *Restoring the Christian Soul through Healing Prayer* (Wheaton, IL: Crossway, 1991), 32.
2. Louis Harris, *Inside America* (New York: Vintage Books, 1987).
3. Tim LaHaye, *How to Win over Depression* (Grand Rapids: Zondervan, 1974), 141.
4. Raymond McHenry, *The Best of In Other Words* (Author, 1996), 22–23.
5. As told to this author by Dr. James Michaelson.
6. Compiled from several sources, including Brian Meehan, "Softball Opponents Offer Unique Display of Sportsmanship," *The Oregonian*, April 29, 2008.

NOTES

Chapter 11: Pessimism

1. "What Flows Beneath," *Los Angeles Times*, August 21, 2000.
2. King Duncan, *Amusing Grace* (Knoxville, TN: Seven Worlds, 1993), 269.

Chapter 12: Anger

1. Anthony Campolo, *Seven Deadly Sins* (Wheaton, IL: Victor Books, 1987).
2. *The Voice of the Village*, July/August 1996.

Chapter 13: Rejection

1. *Our Daily Bread* (Grand Rapids: Radio Bible Class Ministries,).

Chapter 16: Depression

1. See Ron Lee Davis, *Courage to Begin Again* (Eugene, OR: Harvest House, 1988), 54–55.
2. Michael Jacobson, "Stress and the Heart," October 1996.
3. *Our Daily Bread* (Grand Rapids: Radio Bible Class Ministries,).
4. Cited in *The Saturday Evening Post,* September–October 1992, 61.

Chapter 17: Envy

1. *Preaching,* May–June 1997, 58.
2. Ted Kyle and John Todd, ed., *A Treasury of Bible Illustrations* (Chattanooga, TN: AMG, 1995), 165.
3. Ed Diener, *The Futurist,* University of Illinois at Urbana-Champaign, Office of Public Affairs, News Bureau, November–December 1993, 7.
4. Ibid.
5. BBC News, February 12, 2001.

Chapter 18: Jealousy

1. Charles Swindoll, *The Tale of the Tardy Oxcart* (Nashville: Word, 1998), 311.
2. Paul Tan, *Encyclopedia of 7700 Illustrations* (Rockville, MD: Assurance, 1979), 646.
3. BBC News, April 19, 2000.
4. Ralph Earle, *Word Meanings in the New Testament* (Peabody, MA: Hendrickson, 1997), 239.

Chapter 19: Discouragement

1. *Our Daily Bread* (Grand Rapids: Radio Bible Class Ministries, May 17, 1989).

Chapter 20: Death

1. "Fish Kills Man," Associated Press, March 8, 1988.

2. "Snake Shoots Man to Death," Associated Press, April 24, 1990.

3. Sheila Rule, "Fan Hurt by Model Plane at Halftime at Shea Dies," *New York Times*, December 15, 1979.

4. "Monkeys Stone Herder in Kenya," Associated Press, February 24, 2000.

5. Cited in Paul Carlson, *Before I Wake* (Elgin, IL: David C. Cook, 1975), 143.

6. Jan Barclay, *Living and Enjoying the Fruit of the Spirit* (Chicago: Moody Press, 1976), 14–15.

7. Brian Harbour, *Brian's Lines*, February 1992.